RETHINKING TAXATION
AN INTRODUCTION TO
HOURLY AVERAGING

Published under licence 2012 by Searching Finance Ltd.

ISBN: 978-1-907720-92-5

Typeset and designed by Deirdré Gyenes

RETHINKING TAXATION
AN INTRODUCTION TO
HOURLY AVERAGING

Douglas Bamford

Searching
finance

About the author

Douglas received his PhD from the Politics and International Studies Department at the University of Warwick in 2013 for his thesis entitled *Egalitarian Taxation*.

He has presented his work at international conferences and along with this book has had papers published in edited collections and in an academic journal.

His blog is called "Doug Bamford's Tax Appeal" and can be found at http://dougstaxappeal.blogspot.co.uk/.

Doug supports Nottingham Forest FC and is a native of Reading, UK.

About Searching Finance

Searching Finance Ltd is a dynamic new voice in knowledge provision for the financial services and related professional sectors. For more information, please visit www.searchingfinance.com.

CONTENTS

Preface and Acknowledgements ix

Introduction 1
The features by which to judge tax systems 4
Outline of the book.. 8

Part I 11
Chapter one: The hourly averaging calculation 13
Traditional lifetime averaging 14
Hourly averaging 17
The special role of hour credits in the calculation 20
Examples 22
Subsidy rates 26
Tax rates...29
Conclusion 33

Chapter two: Hour credits... 35
Source and nature of hour credits......................................36
Hour credits for the disabled 37
Involuntary unemployment and the guaranteed work
     programme...38
Additional hour credits: Students and carers 41
Maximum hour credits..44
Hour credit fines...46
Life without hour credits in an hour credit society....................47
Conclusion 49

Chapter three: Why introduce hourly averaging? 51
Principles of taxation 51

Who is better-off and who is worse-off with hourly
    averaging? 53
Effective redistribution 57
Economic incentives 66
Hourly averaging and economic efficiency 69
Conclusion 73

Part II 75
Chapter four: the tax base 77
Wage income or a comprehensive tax base? 78
Comprehensive tax bases 81
The acquired income tax base 84
Determining "gains" 87
Calculating acquired income 91
Obtaining information on acquired income 94
Conclusion 97

Chapter five: Lifetime averaging 99
Beginnings 100
Reaching majority 103
Adulthood and inflation 104
Merging and demerging accounts 106
Retirement and pensions 108
Death 111
Conclusion 112

Part III 115
Chapter six: Constitutional requirements 117
Would the CLIPH-rate tax cause macroeconomic damage? 118
The Constitution of a Sovereign Wealth Fund 120
Abuse of power and government as Leviathan 122
Limits on government agencies 125
The power of those who confer hour credits 127
Conclusion 128

Chapter seven: Anti-fraud measures 131
Responding to fraud 132
Rule setting 135
Information gathering 138
Computer-based checks 141
Employers and employees of particular concern 143

CONTENTS

Investigations and prosecutions 147
Advantages of hour credits and acquired income 149
Conclusion 151

Chapter eight: Transitional conditions....................................... **153**
International tax competition 154
Compatible international ecosystems 156
The ideal ecosystem: fair global taxation...........................159
Practicalities of transition: Setting up the systems 164
New and Altered Institutions 166
Past information 168
Conclusion 170

Conclusion...**173**
Reason for optimism?..173

Appendix **175**

Endnotes **179**

Index...**197**

TABLES AND FIGURES

Table 1.1: Monthly figures 23
Table 1.2: One hundredth month calculation 24
Table 1.3: One hundredth month calculation after a windfall 25
Table 4.1: Individual level of taxation.................................80
Table 4.2: Investment outlay, returns and taxation 90

Figure 1.1: Negative tax rates on low average hourlyincomes 27
Figure 1.2: Hourly net income subsidy................................27
Figure 1.3: Smooth curve (logarithmic)..............................30
Figure 1.4: Smooth graph with kink....................................31
Figure 1.5: Straight-line graph with kink 31
Figure 1.6: Straight-line graph......................................31
Figure 1.7: Curved graph with kink around 0% tax point 32
Figure 1.8: Net income always rises when gross income does 32
Figure 1.9: Net income increases with kinked graph 33

PREFACE AND ACKNOWLEDGMENTS

I FIRST had the idea that the most appropriate view of taxation would be based on an hour of work when I was studying for an MA around nine years ago. This has seemed obvious to me since that moment and I hope that I have produced a work that will convince others of the idea. I would firstly like to thank my parents, Moira and Peter, for their unwavering love and support during the many years I have been working towards the publication of the ideas contained in this book. My Grandparents and brother, Dan, have also been very supportive and understanding of me as I've put my all into developing and articulating this idea.

I have received much moral and emotional support from friends during this time. I feel should mention Helen Jackson, Rowena Viney, Mark Harrison, Nathan Lyons, Martin Curtis, Wendy Muirhead, and Anne Rawson. I owe a particular debt of gratitude to my two closest friends Sam Wade and Olly Murray.

Along the way, I have discussed my proposal with various people and would like to mention a few whose comments or other forms of support I greatly appreciate; Kaz Morii, Alex Sutton, Chris Clarke, Louise Walker, Andy Walton, Stephen Morris, Liz Kingston and Alex Twiggs. I would also like to thank my publisher, Ashwin Rattan who offered me the chance to write this book for him and for his advice on its format. Several people have assisted me by reading through chapters of the book; Sebastian Bosely, Matt Fernandez, Attiya Waris, and Sam Wade.

In order to improve my ability to express my ideas, and to be taken more seriously, I undertook a PhD at Warwick University. I would like to thank my supervisors, Matthew Clayton and Andrew Reeve for their patience in guiding me through that process and dragging me through it. Liam Shields began his thesis at the same time as I did, though was always far ahead and inevitably finished much before me. He has provided me with a lot of useful advice and comments, both on my thesis and several chapters of this book. Lastly, but no doubt mostly, I thank Katy Long for her support, patience, and understanding—as well as her valued advice—while I have worked on this subject.

DOUG BAMFORD
June 2013

INTRODUCTION

GOVERNMENTS need taxation revenues in order to pay for the basic functions of the state, such as the military, police, and the justice system. However, taxation has another important role; that of ensuring an appropriate distribution of resources in society. Some people would claim that an unconstrained market would produce an appropriate distribution of resources.[1] However, this is clearly false. Markets work very well for a fortunate few and less well for the less fortunate, and it is not fair to have an economic system that works much better for some than others. Taxation and transfer policies are therefore needed in order to correct this market luck and ensure a fair distribution of resources.

However, a major problem with attempts to tax the economically fortunate and improve the position of the less fortunate is that these attempts can discourage people from working. If the fortunate face a high tax rate they may decide to work less and enjoy more leisure—since much of their additional earnings are taxed anyway. If the less fortunate receive income subsidies or other benefits, then they may also take the opportunity to work less and enjoy more leisure. This issue has led to regular and on-going public debates about the welfare system and the deserving and undeserving poor. Economists refer to this as substitution of leisure for income. Discouraging work can diminish the positive benefits of taxation and programmes to assist the poor as it can reduce the overall effectiveness of the economy, affect prices, and cause a greater number of people to require assistance. This book contains a proposal for a system that would tax the fortunate in order to help the less fortunate *without* the unwanted side-effect of creating work disincentives.

I have labelled the tax system I propose here the *CLIPH-rate tax*. This stands for Comprehensive Lifetime Income Per-hour-rate. This proposal contains two components, which can be separated, but work best when put together. The major innovation of the proposal is *hourly averaging*. This is the proposal to calculate a lifetime tax rate for each taxpayer on the basis of their average *hourly income*. The idea of taxing people on a lifetime average basis is not a new one. However, previous proposals calculated averages based upon the amount of time passed. The *hourly* averaging proposal, however, relates to the amount of time the taxpayer has spent in work during their life, utilising what I call hour credits. People would obtain *hour credits* from spending time working, which would put work at the heart of the economic system.

The main focus of this book is to explain the new form of hourly tax calculation, though in chapter four I will present the other novel component of the CLIPH-rate tax. This is the Comprehensive Income parts of the acronym, as I propose a new form of comprehensive income tax base. I also refer to this new comprehensive tax base as *acquired income*. This is a hybrid of consumption and comprehensive income tax bases, and works well with lifetime hourly averaging to generate a fair tax system. The two components are separable, but in the later chapters I will mostly discuss them together.

One challenge to a radical new tax proposal such as this is whether it is feasible. Indeed, it is plausible that others have previously invented hourly averaging but dismissed the idea as utopian. However, just with other areas which have been recently reimagined or revolutionised by new technology, so technological advances have rendered feasible this proposal for a fundamental redesign of taxation. Many aspects of our lives and economy have been transformed by the increasing availability of cheap computer power, electronic data storage, and instantaneous electronic communication. These technologies make it possible to improve the fairness and efficiency of the tax system just as they have allowed us to have a video-conference with someone on the other side of the world, or pay bills, or buy and read books online.

There are three ways in which technology makes lifetime averaging and an acquired income tax base much more feasible. First, it enables us to conceive systems of instantaneous tax calculation using computer technology. This means that it is possible to undertake more complex calculations at more regular intervals and get them right each time. Indeed, "real-time taxation" is being introduced in the UK at the time of writing. Second, the tax system and financial payment systems could be *integrated* with real-time taxation calculations, such that the correct tax is withheld from all transactions at source.[2] This enables more complex calculations to occur automatically and without any difficulty for taxpayers. Third, we can imagine people interacting regularly and conveniently with a tax authority website, updating their information and ascertaining their latest tax rate—and predicted future tax rate—at their convenience. This makes personal taxation simpler for taxpayers and governments, as well as increasing the reliability of tax returns. My focus here will not be on the technological possibilities; I will assume those to be available.

Of course, that something is possible does not mean it should be done. The tax system should be reformed or replaced if the changes are morally preferable to the current system and the available alternatives. I will not attempt to justify the morality of the system in this book.[3] However, I will provide some basic criteria for judging the tax system in the following section. For the purposes of this work I will make the relatively uncontroversial assumption that the tax system should—among other things—redistribute resources from the economically fortunate to the economically unfortunate. The advantage of the CLIPH-rate tax is that it achieves these aims much more successfully than other tax and transfer policies. Furthermore, it would create fewer and less serious side-effects while doing so.

The features by which to judge tax systems

The choice of a tax and benefit system is inherently normative, and so should be judged from the best available theory of distributive justice from political philosophy. The most attractive approach is Ronald Dworkin's resource egalitarianism. This supports property rights and free exchange as long as everyone begins from a suitably equal position. In our society, since we do not start with equal talents and family backgrounds, Dworkin proposes *hypothetical insurance*.[4]

The hypothetical insurance procedure models redistribution from the fortunate to the unfortunate based upon people's views of the costs and benefits of the redistribution to the fortunate and unfortunate. People would be asked what form and level of redistribution they would choose if they did not know whether they were among the fortunate or less fortunate. Asking people to choose as if they did not know whether they were going to pay out or receive enables them to consider the costs and risks, just as people do when considering insurance packages in the real world. So people are asked what tax and benefit system they would choose if they did not know whether they were from a rich or poor background, whether they have good or bad random fortune in their investments, and whether or not they had talents that enabled them to find well-paid work—or any work at all—in their society. As people would choose the level of redistribution from a position of equality where they do not know their level of economic fortune, the system that would follow would show equal concern for all.

However, I will not argue for any particular normative underpinnings nor defend the hypothetical insurance approach in this book. My aim is to present a new approach to taxation and redistribution. However, it is necessary to say something about the features that a good tax system should have, and so I will list some here. The features I will set out are those that I think hypothetical insurers would choose, but they will also be attractive to those who wish to judge taxation according to a different theory.[5] Many of the elements of a good tax system I will present were described by Adam Smith in his *Wealth of Nations*.[6] However, as is clear from what I have said above, I would replace his vague notion of equity with a more developed theory of distributive justice.

The first feature of a good tax system is that it should distribute resources appropriately among the members of society. Specifically, it should redistribute from the economically fortunate to the less fortunate. The most clearly fortunate are those who receive windfalls, such as gifts and bequests from family members. However, some people have talents which they can convert into skills that enable them to command substantial premiums in a market economy; classic examples are footballing skills in a society in which football teams have turnovers in the region of £100m a year or, mathematical talents that are valued within the finance industry. Many features that influence people's careers may come from differences in genetics or nurturing while an infant. These disadvantages are clearly matters of luck about which people bear no responsibility. Thus the tax system should seek to increase the resources of the less fortunate, ideally by taxing the more fortunate rather than those with average fortune.[7] Income does not only correspond with fortune, of course, as some people will earn more than others with the same fortune by working harder or in less popular work. However, there is often a correlation, and so there is a need for progressive taxation, particularly where this tracks fortune as closely as possible.[8]

RETHINKING TAXATION:
AN INTRODUCTION TO HOURLY AVERAGING

The tax system must raise the revenue required in order to improve the situation of the less fortunate, but there are many additional crucial government functions that require revenue. These include democratic institutions, the legal system, national defence, health care, education, foreign aid,[9] and environmental and economic regulation. A lot of revenue is required, and the greater the proportion of this that comes from the more economically fortunate rather than the less fortunate the better.

The second feature of a good tax system is that it should not restrict people in living their lives. In one sense, of course, when someone pays taxes they will as a result have fewer resources to live their lives than they might have had under an alternative tax system. However, this difference is not a restriction that should worry us, as long as the taxes are just. The restrictions I mean to rule out are those that a tax policy would cause if it forced some people to do work that others in society are not forced to do. This rules out taxation calculated on the *endowment*, or *ability*, that taxpayers have.[10] Endowment taxes of this kind will mean that those with rare and valuable skills will be forced to use them while others can choose their job and hours. If people wish to use these endowments, then so much the better and it is perfectly acceptable to tax them more as a result. However, it is not right to force people to use their particular skills and talents.

Adam Smith's principles are useful in determining a third feature of a good tax system. This is that the system should be convenient to taxpayers and stable. These two aspects are linked, since a stable system which does not change constantly will be more convenient to taxpayers.[11] The requirement of a convenient tax system has further implications. Taxpayers should not have too much of their time and energy taken up by the requirements of paying their taxes. I will not discuss this issue at too much length, despite the worry that the system proposed here would require more effort from taxpayers. I will assume that the judicious use of IT systems can reduce this burden on taxpayers to enable a sufficiently convenient system that is superior in the other respects to the current scheme and other proposed alternatives.

The fourth and final feature is that the system should not have detrimental economic effects. Taxation is certain to affect the economy but some effects are particularly unwanted. The tax system should not damage the prospects of economic development and growth.[12] One way for it to avoid this is to keep the *marginal* and *participation* tax rates low. Marginal tax rates are the tax rates that relate to the decision that a taxpayer makes, since they are the rate that applies to the next pound that they will earn. So if someone is deciding whether to work an hour of overtime, he will consider whether it is worth doing so given the 50% tax rate that he will pay on this overtime income and ignore the fact that his average tax rate is 32%. While someone might have a low or high average tax rate overall, what will affect their decision is the marginal tax rate they face on the action they are considering. The marginal rate may cause someone to refuse additional work since the gain to them is mostly taxed away.

An important effect that has only been emphasised more recently is that of the participation tax rate.[13] There may be occasions—the common example used is unemployment benefit, but it equally applies to retirement choices—whereby people feel they are no better-off overall if they work compared to not working. If the incentives to work are reduced due to tax or benefit policies, then many people will work less or not at all. This will have detrimental consequences for investors and consumers (and we are all consumers), since trades that would have benefitted them will not happen or will cost them more.

It is valuable to highlight an intersection between the first and fourth criteria. These seem to be opposed to one another, as high tax rates may have detrimental economic effects. However, this is not always the case. High tax rates on *windfalls* (inheritance, gifts, capital gains) or *rents*—returns on the ownership of something in limited supply such as a rare talent or land—are *not economically damaging* since they do not tend to alter economic choices. Indeed, if anything, taxing windfalls will reduce the scope for there to be a "leisure-class"[14] or "idle-rich" who can live a comfortable existence without contributing to the economy. Windfalls and rents should not be taxed at 100%, as they do provide indirect incentives: for people to build up wealth or a company to generate a windfall for themselves or others. Furthermore, there should be some scope for people to improve the lives of their loved ones to a degree. Just to be clear, these rents are also available to those who have valuable talents. It is hard to imagine many professional footballers who would give up their careers if they were taxed at much higher rates; many people are willing to pay to play the game—including me!

Taxing those who receive large windfalls at highly progressive rates should not affect economic activity too much nor affect the prospects of the vast majority of society, while providing important revenue. A tax system that can capture such windfalls effectively will be an attractive one. The hourly averaging proposal presented here is able to do this, which is one of the several advantages of the system I will describe.

Outline of the book

I have divided the book into three parts: the basics of hourly averaging, an explanation of further details of the system including the acquired comprehensive income tax base, and finally the practical issues that need to be overcome in order to introduce the system. The aim of this book is to explain lifetime hourly averaging and to indicate why it is a superior system of taxation and benefit payment. It is superior because the system effectively taxes the economically fortunate and assists the less fortunate with minimal economic side-effects. The first part provides the basic answers to these questions. I begin with a chapter explaining how this calculation works. Hour credits are a crucial element of the calculation and are the novel feature of the system. Therefore, I describe the nature of hour credits in chapter two and explain some of their interesting features. In the third chapter I explain why calculating tax in this way is better than the alternatives.

Part two provides further details of the CLIPH-rate tax system. A tax calculation must be applied to a specific tax base and in chapter four I will consider this important issue. I explain which forms of tax base are compatible with lifetime hourly averaging, and express my preference for the acquired income tax base. Chapter five provides more detail on the calculation of taxation over the lifetime of an individual. I therefore explain the beginnings and ends of the individual's account. I also explain how it would be possible for couples to merge their tax accounts when they merge their other affairs together, and how the system would account for inflation.

The final part of the book outlines some further details of the system while responding to potential challenges. Chapter six presents further features that the system would require under the heading of constitutional issues. These arise out of various potential challenges to the system regarding the power that certain parties could wield if they were not constrained. In chapter seven I discuss the increased scope for fraud afforded through the introduction of hour credits, and I explain how to counter these additional forms of fraud. The expense of the additional anti-fraud measures are well worth the cost given the advantages of the system overall.

The final chapter considers the practicalities of transitioning to an hourly averaging system. These primarily arise due to the nature of state-based taxation in a globalised world, but I will also indicate the transitional steps to an hourly system. It would take huge political will to convert the global tax system in order to facilitate hourly averaging. The aim of this book is to show that hourly averaging is not only attractive but also a viable option.

PART I

CHAPTER ONE

THE HOURLY AVERAGING

CALCULATION

IN THE FIRST part of the book I will outline the basic features of hourly averaging and explain why it is a superior system. In the first chapter I will set out how to calculate taxation on a lifetime hourly average basis. I will also present the kinds of progressive tax rates that should be utilised as part of the system. In chapter two I will give a more detailed explanation of hour credits, which are a necessary part of the calculation system. I will explain what they are and what people would need to do in order to obtain them. In the third chapter I will argue that hourly averaging better meets the features of a good tax system than its rival systems.

Most of the taxes that have applied to persons, rather than particular kinds of transactions or particular items of property, have been applied on an annual basis. The current UK tax system, for example, calculates income taxation and national insurance on the basis of the amount of money earned in each tax year. Each tax year is entirely separate and has no bearing on any other. In this chapter I will explain how to calculate taxation on a lifetime hourly average basis.

The idea of *lifetime* tax averaging is not new, and in the first section I will outline this idea. I will then explain that instead of dividing by a period of time such as years, hourly averaging would divide that lifetime tax base by the number of hour credits that the taxpayer in question has had recorded. I will say more about hour credits in chapter two, but in this chapter I will explain the crucial role that they play in the calculation. The role of hour credits is further borne out when I explain the different ways that taxpayers could view the effect that hour credits have on their taxation and their income. I will provide some illustrative examples throughout, but the middle section of this chapter is particularly devoted to examples.

Hourly averaging allows much more progressive taxation than other tax systems, and in the final two sections I present graphs which indicate the kind of tax rates that would be attractive. In the penultimate section I explain how negative hourly tax rates can be applied to low earners. This is because the hourly averaging calculation can be utilised as a form of earnings subsidy for low-earners. It can therefore replace, or partially replace, other policies such as the minimum wage and pre-existing tax credits. Hourly averaging provides a very attractive way of assisting the less economically fortunate, as well as a more effective means to tax the more fortunate. In the final section I present graphs of the tax rates that would be applied on an hourly average basis.

Traditional lifetime averaging

The idea of averaging income[15] for tax purposes has a long heritage and multiple-year "moving" averaging has been introduced on several occasions around the world.[16] This is because law-makers have recognised that a year is an arbitrary amount of time on which to determine someone's tax rate. Progressive taxation on annual incomes will fall more heavily on those who have highly fluctuating incomes.[17] In the good years those with a fluctuating income will pay a lot of tax while in the bad years they pay little tax but also receive little income. This uses the tax system to smooth out income over time, so that sudden changes in gross income will have a less immediate effect.

Due to the downsides of multiple-year averaging,[18] a more principled lifetime averaging approach has been discussed since its advocacy in the 1930s and 40s by U.S. economist William Vickrey.[19] Despite this advocacy, however, *lifetime averaging* has never been introduced anywhere.

Vickrey's calculation involves *cumulative averaging*. This means that someone who had been taxed for five years would have her total income over that period applied to a five-year tax rate table, and there would be similar cumulative tables for people who had been taxed for four years, six years, and so on. Our taxpayer would apply her cumulative taxable income to the relevant (five-year) tax rate table to determine how much tax she should have paid up until this point in her life. In order to calculate her current tax liability she would subtract her past tax payments from this new total and pay the tax authority the difference.

It is straightforward enough to replace this cumulative approach involving numerous tax-tables with a *true averaging* formula which would divide total lifetime income by the time period in order to calculate an average annual income. True averaging would enable the application of a single average tax rate schedule to all taxpayers. In order to calculate her tax liability, our five-year taxpayer would split this gross annual average into an annual tax average. She would then multiply this tax average by the number of years—five—to see the amount of tax she should now have paid in total. She would then deduct her past tax payments from this new total in order to calculate her current liability. All past payments would need to be adjusted for inflation, which would be done automatically by the tax authority, as I will describe in chapter five.

To show the advantage of averaging, consider an example involving a business-owner, James, whose business has grown over a number of years. If there are progressive *annual* taxes,

then his sale of the business will—we can reasonably assume—
be taxed at the highest rate. He may therefore choose to sell
parts of the business over a number of years in order to qualify for a lower rate. This would be bad for James and bad for
the potential buyers, since they would not make the deal they
would have liked to make for the entire business.

The usual attempt to avoid this situation is to separate
capital gains from regular income taxation and to offer lower
taxes on capital gains. Ideally, however, capital gains should be
taxed at a *higher* rate than taxes on labour, as capital gains are
more of a windfall and would not produce labour disincentives. Furthermore, reducing the rate of tax on capital gains
makes the tax system less progressive, meaning that those who
earn their money through capital gains would pay much less in
tax than those who earn the same amount of money as regular income. Progressive annual taxes, then, lead to inefficiency
if they include capital gains and will be unfair if they do not.
Where taxes are calculated on a *lifetime* basis, however, James
can sell his business when he likes without any tax considerations as the income will be applied to his lifetime income. The
tax on the gain will be spread out over the many years he has
been working on the business, and the gain will continue to
benefit him for the rest of his working life. I will explain how
this works in greater detail in the remainder of this chapter.
The important point to note, however, is that progressive taxes
can be applied on lifetime income without the inefficiency and
unfairness that would apply where they applied to each year
separately.

Consider the further examples of windfall-recipients and
those with different career-paths. Those receiving windfalls
may do so evenly over the course of their lives, but most windfall-recipients receive a few large windfalls at various points in
their lives—for example when a relative dies. It is much more
common for workers to receive a steady income over their lives
although this is by no means universal. Some jobs—such as

medical doctors—require years of unpaid or low-paid training, followed by a relatively highly-paid career. Other people
have careers whereby they start at a relatively low position in
their field or company and work their way into specialist or
high-responsibility positions. Self-employed workers are also
more likely to have variable incomes: they often have to build
up their reputations within their field, and sometimes have to
spend a lot of time creating their product—for example, artists
or musicians—or updating their skills through re-training—
for example, technology consultants.[20] Another example is
that of time-limited careers, such as professional sportspeople
who can earn large sums in their twenties and thirties but then
retire with uncertain prospects. Lifetime taxation is fairer to
people with these careers and windfalls.

Lifetime averaging enables us to distinguish those with
consistently high windfalls or income—and therefore good
fortune—from those with a *temporarily* high income—who
may not have such good fortune overall. It therefore more effectively distinguishes between the highly fortunate and those
who are not so highly fortunate. This enables higher tax rates
on those with high lifetime earnings, without fear of excessive
impact upon those with temporarily high income or a one-off
large windfall.[21] There are further advantages of moving from
time-passed-based to hour-credit-based averaging.

Hourly averaging

Hourly averaging does not utilise time passed but rather *hours
credited.*[22] The idea here is that people would obtain an hour
credit for each hour of work they perform for a registered
employer[23] and that these hour credits would form the basis
of the averaging calculation. Employers would inform the tax
authority of the number of hours that each worker has been
paid for working in the specified period.[24] These hour credits
would take the place of years or months in time-passed-based

averaging calculations, with each person's *total lifetime gross income* divisible instead by their total number of hour credits to determine an *average hourly gross value.*

Tax rates are applied on this *average hourly gross income* of the taxpayer in accordance with the tax rate graph that applies to all taxpayers. The gross average is then split into a net and tax portion in accordance with this tax rate, which determines the amount of tax that each person should pay on every hour's gross income. Another way to put this is that the hourly gross amount is split into a tax portion and a net income portion, which indicates the amount that the taxpayer can keep. This split is true by definition since tax and net income add up to gross income. These amounts all refer to hourly averages but the individual's tax payments are determined on the basis of their lifetime totals.

Lifetime averaging works by treating each point in time as if each payment will be the last payment by (and to) the taxpayer.[25] There is no need to anticipate future income or hour credits. It is possible to calculate the amount of lifetime tax that the individual should have paid and net income received up to the present. This is achieved by multiplying the hourly tax and net-income figures by the number of hour credits. These totals then indicate the amount of tax that the individual should have paid to the government and the net amount that they should have received up until that point. So to work out the amount of tax that an individual should pay in the present period it is necessary to calculate the amount of tax that she should have paid in her entire lifetime and then deduct the amount that she has paid up to that point. The difference between the two figures indicates her current tax liability.

As I have said, gross income equals net income plus taxation, and this fact applies both on an hourly and lifetime basis; accordingly, lifetime taxation plus lifetime net income will equal lifetime gross income. Therefore, it is possible to focus on the *lifetime net income that a taxpayer should have received*

up to the present rather than the *tax that they should have paid.*
The result will be the same, since if the taxpayer has received
the correct lifetime net income she will have also paid the
correct lifetime tax.

The process works by regularly ensuring that each taxpayer
has paid the lifetime tax and received the lifetime net income
that she should have done, given three considerations: her
gross lifetime income, how many hour credits she has, and the
tax rate graph that applies in her society. This calculation can
be done as often as desired, for example once a week or month,
but modern IT systems should be able to withhold the correct
taxation at every single transaction.[26] Each time the procedure occurs as if it were to be the last payment on the person's
account. Some readers may find it easier to understand the
steps of the calculation if it is expressed in equations and so
I have included these as an appendix. Other readers will find
examples more helpful and so I will present one here.

Sarah (conveniently) has a fifty per cent tax rate. Up until
now, Sarah had received 9,825 hour credits and a gross income
of £255,450. In the past month she has worked 175 hours and
received £4,550, so Sarah has now worked 10,000 hours, earning £260,000. As she has a fifty per cent tax rate, Sarah should
now have paid £130,000 in tax and received £130,000 in net
income. In this simple example, Sarah had previously received
£127,725 net income and paid that amount in tax. Her additional 175 hours and £4,550 therefore nets her £2,275 income
this month, which—since her tax rate is fifty per cent—is
also her tax bill. This example is straightforward—not much
happens since Sarah's tax rate stays the same. However, the
example does show the process of calculating current tax
liability. I will present further examples in a later section in
this chapter featuring taxpayers whose rates do change.

The special role of hour credits in the calculation

Hourly averaging is not particularly complicated. However, it does work somewhat differently from other forms of taxation. It is therefore useful to emphasise the role that hour credits would play in tax calculations. I will do this firstly by presenting an extreme example that should illustrate how important hour credits are to taxpayers under an hourly system. In order to make the role of hour credits clearer I will explain towards the end of this section the different ways that taxpayers might view hour credits.

In order to make the extreme illustrative example, I will assume that *all* income is accounted for according to the hourly system, no matter what its source. This anticipates *the comprehensive acquired income* tax base I will propose in chapter four, though I will explain in that chapter that hourly averaging need not be applied in such a comprehensive manner. The example is of a teenager, Tom, who obtains a large windfall income prior to the acquisition of any hour credits. Imagine that Tom's Grandparents give him one million pounds. I will discuss the treatment of children and the nature of lifetime taxation in further detail in chapter five, but for now let us assume that income directed at children will go into their budding tax account.

The example is extreme because Tom will have his entire windfall taxed in the first instance. This is because he has no hour credits. We might say that his average hourly income is infinity as it is divided by zero and that this should be taxed at one hundred per cent. However, less controversially, we can say that his net hourly income is irrelevant since whatever it is will be multiplied by zero hour credits to determine his lifetime income. Any positive number multiplied by zero will be zero, and so his lifetime net income must be zero. If the computer system were to struggle with the existence of zeros in the calculation then it would be possible to provide everyone with a single hour credit and a small amount of money in their account before it comes into effect. However, even if we allow for this, Tom will have a very high gross hourly income and a very high tax rate.

Now consider Maude, who also receives a one million pound windfall. However, she receives her bequest at the age of sixty and has already built up a lot of hour credits on her tax account. Let us say that her lifetime tax rate after the bequest is seventy per cent. Maude will receive £300,000 upon the bequest, while it may appear that Tom receives nothing upon his receipt. However, this is to overlook the dynamism of the system. In fact the two recipients are in similar positions. This is because Tom will receive hour credits during his life—after all he will have to in order to obtain any income. Every time Tom receives an hour credit his unusually large gross income will be divided by a larger number of hour credits, thus bringing down his gross hourly average income. This drop in gross hourly average will in turn result in a drop in his lifetime tax rate. As his lifetime tax rate drops, Tom will receive a larger and larger portion of his large gross lifetime income. Another way to understand this is that Tom's bequest will *gradually* be released to him as he obtains hour credits.

By the time he reaches the age of sixty, all else being the same, Tom will have received the same amount of his bequest as Maude: £300,000. Of course, one difference is that Tom will have received it over the course of his working life, while Maude will receive the net amount at once. However, if they both continue to obtain hour credits, they will continue to receive more with each additional credit than they would have had if they never received the bequest.

These extreme examples indicate that taxpayers can view hour credits and income in various ways which would help them to anticipate their future income. Taxpayers would receive net income either when they obtain gross income or when they obtain hour credits. Of course they therefore receive net income when they obtain gross income and hour credits together. This means that taxpayers can guess their future income reasonably accurately given their past figures. When someone receives an hour credit, they know that it will be worth a certain amount of net income (£x) for them. Alternatively, when someone receives an amount of gross income, they will know that their lifetime tax rate is currently y per cent and that they will receive this proportion of their gross income.

In this way, most taxpayers could make reasonably accurate calculations of their future income based on their knowledge of the basics of their lifetime tax account. Some people will not be able to rely on such simple calculations, of course, due to the large changes that will happen to their hourly average as their situation changes. This is what happens in extreme cases such as that of Tom and Maude. In his early adulthood, Tom's lifetime gross average will change greatly with each of his additional hour credits, and so his tax rate and returns to hour credits will change over time. Maude will also have a large change upon receipt of her bequest since this will greatly increase her tax rate. So rather than her previously usual twenty per cent tax rate on gross income, Maude would pay seventy per cent on her large windfall.

Examples

Angela and Bertrand are talented individuals who can earn a large amount in the job market—let us say up to £25 an hour. Cassandra and Derek, on the other hand, have more limited options and can only obtain work that pays £6 per hour. Bertrand and Derek are leisure-lovers, as they wish to read novels. They therefore desire only the income necessary to survive and obtain novels, which we will assume to be £6,000 a year (£500 a month). Cassandra and Angela desire to work full-time and earn whatever they can from that. Let us assume that these numbers have held constant for their entire working lives, and that they have received no outside income. In their society, the tax on a £6 gross average is zero, while the tax on £25 is sixty per cent. This allows us to create the following table for each month.

Table 1.1: Monthly figures

	Gross Income	Hour Credits	Hourly Average	Tax Rate	Net hourly	Net Income
Angela	£4,000	160	£25	60%	£10	£1,600
Bertrand	£1,250	50	£25	60%	£10	£500
Cassandra	£960	160	£6	0%	£6	£960
Derek	£504	84	£6	0%	£6	£504

The system works by treating each point in time as if it will be the last payment by (and to) the taxpayer.[27] It is possible to calculate the amount of tax that the individual should have paid and net income received up to the present. These totals are then used to calculate current liabilities. To illustrate this, imagine the individuals above have reached their hundredth month of work, represented in table 1.2. The net income due to the individual at the latest point is easily calculated by subtracting past total net receipts from 99 months (*) from the current amounts due after 100 (**).[28] Since in the simplified example the individuals have had a consistent average hourly income level their net income does not change, and it is the same in the hundredth month as it was in their first.

Table 1.2: One hundredth month calculation

	Previous Gross total	Prev. H/C total	Prev. Net total *	
Angela	£396,000	15840	£158,400	
Bertrand	£123,750	4950	£49,500	
Cassandra	£95,040	15840	£95,040	
Derek	£49,896	8316	£49,896	
	New Gross total	New H/C total	New Net total **	New Net Income
Angela	£400,000	16000	£160,000	£1600
Bertrand	£125,000	5000	£50,000	£500
Cassandra	£96,000	16000	£96,000	£960
Derek	£50,400	8400	£50,400	£504

The examples above show how the calculation works for individuals in the unlikely situation that their economic situation does not change from one month to another. However, in order to provide a more dynamic example, imagine that each individual also receives a £50,000 windfall in their hundredth month. Again, assuming that windfall income is included as part of a comprehensive tax base, this will increase the tax rate of the individuals. Furthermore, it will increase the tax rate of the part-time workers more than that of the full-time workers.

Table 1.3: One hundredth month calculation after a windfall

	Previous Gross total	Prev. H/C total	Prev. Net total *
Angela	£396,000	15,840	£158,400
Bertrand	£123,750	4,950	£49,500
Cassandra	£95,040	15,840	£95,040
Derek	£49,896	8,316	£49,896

	New Gross total	New H/C total	New Tax rate	New Net total **	New Net Income
Angela	£450,000	16,000	64%	£162,000	£3,600
Bertrand	£175,000	5,000	71%	£50,750	£1,500
Cassandra	£146,000	16,000	15%	£124,100	£29,060
Derek	£100,400	8,400	30%	£70,280	£20,384

The windfall affects the tax rates of the part-time workers much more than the full-time workers. This is because it has a greater effect on their lifetime average gross income. In the first month after the windfall, Angela receives an extra £2,000 (4% of the windfall), Bertrand receives £1,000 extra (2%), Cassandra receives an extra £28,100 (56.2%), and Derek receives £19,880 (39.76%). These individuals will continue to benefit from their windfall during future periods, of course, as long as they continue to obtain more hour credits. As time goes on, Angela and Cassandra will benefit most from the windfall, since they will obtain more hour credits. These hour credits will dilute the influence of the windfall on their gross lifetime average income.

In the examples I have given I have simply specified the tax rates that apply to the various individuals. In the following sections I will suggest how the tax rate graph would look that would apply to such individuals.

Subsidy rates

The first part of the calculation to discuss is the element intended to improve the position of those who work but have low pay. There are many proposals to improve the position of the low-paid, such as the minimum wage, a basic income, and various types of earning subsidy. I will compare these approaches to hourly averaging in chapter three. For now, I will explain that hourly averaging opens up the possibility of a novel form of earning subsidy—an income subsidy for those with low average hourly pay. This is an earning subsidy operated through hourly averaging whereby those with a *low hourly average income* should have a *negative tax rate*. This negative rate would top up the income of the low-paid from state funds for each hour credit that they receive.

So if we assume the desirable minimum net income is £6 an hour, those with a gross average of £0.01 would have a negative sixty-thousand per cent tax rate in order to obtain £6 for each hour. Someone with an average gross income of £3.25 an hour might have a negative one hundred per cent tax rate. This would increase their net lifetime average to £6.50, meaning that the state will have paid them £3.25 extra for every hour they work. The tax rate would reach zero, let us say, for those with a £9 average.

The hourly-averaging subsidy would improve the position of those who work in low-paid employment, as an hour of work for them will be worth more than it would otherwise. This is shown by the negative tax rates in Figure 1.1. The subsidy provides the low-paid with more resources or leisure to carry out their plans. The graphs below indicate how the tax rate would apply to those with low lifetime hourly income. As figure 1.2 indicates, net income should always rise with gross income in order to maintain the incentive for people to perform more economically productive labour, while ensuring that those with a very low average would be elevated to a higher hourly income.

Figure 1.1: Negative tax rates on low average hourly incomes

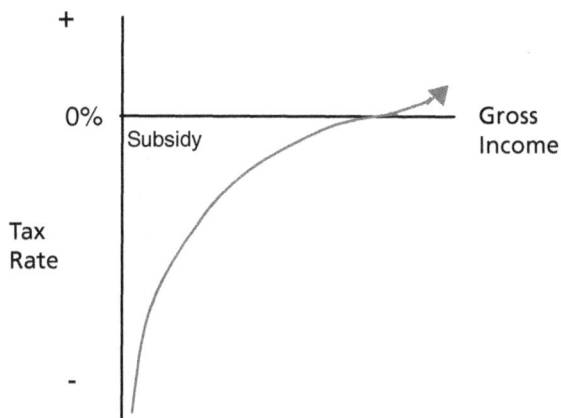

Figure 1.2: Hourly net income subsidy

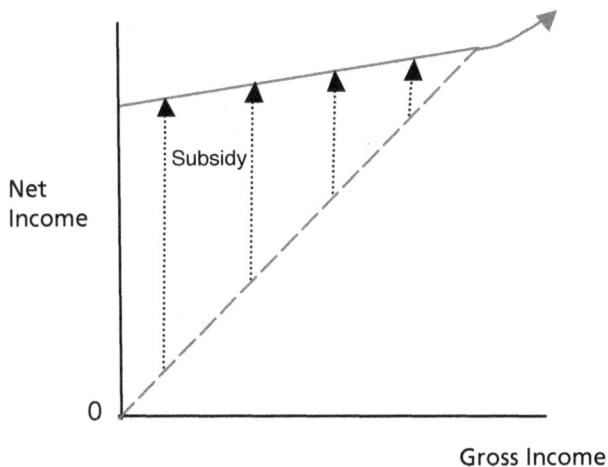

As is perhaps clear, the earnings subsidy element of hourly averaging would remove the need to have a minimum wage at a level sufficient to provide a reasonable standard of living. The earning subsidy would make up the difference for workers who are paid a low gross amount. Workers would receive a reasonable income even if their gross pay was very low. However, I would suggest that a selective minimum wage would be a sensible policy alongside hourly-averaging. This would be *selective* in that it would vary according to *employer* or *job-type*. For most jobs the minimum gross wage could be low (perhaps even £0.01 per hour), but for some jobs it would need to be set at the zero-tax rate level (which was £9 an hour in the example figures given above). The idea is that hour credits for work should not be used to subsidise personal projects and should only be available for work that benefits others, as indicated by economic demand.

Two categories are therefore candidates for higher minimum wage levels. The first category is jobs which are also leisure activities, such as that of professional footballer or artist. People are willing to perform these activities without pay, and so many would happily undertake such work full-time if they would be paid via the earning subsidy to do so, even if no-one else in society would get any substantial benefit from their work. It is therefore necessary to ensure that those gaining hour credits from these jobs are doing the job as a result of a demand for their activities as indicated by the willingness of people (customers, investors, governments, charitable foundations etc.) to pay them to do it.

A second category of jobs that are candidates for a special minimum wage arises since many people are keen to support their preferred political ideology or religion in whatever way they can. I imagine that many people with strong beliefs would work full-time to support their cause, with taxpayer subsidy, if they were able to do so. After all, many people already volunteer in such capacities. As a result, religious and political organizations would be required to pay their workers a higher minimum than profit-seeking firms in order to stop people taking advantage of the subsidies to do work that they would do for free. A selective minimum wage policy would ensure economic efficiency by stopping many people from obtaining social subsidies for their private activities.[29]

Tax rates

I said in the introduction that taxes should be progressive[30] and indeed there is no need to undertake hourly averaging without the desire for progressivity; the advantages of lifetime and hourly averaging only arise where rates are progressive. In this section I will indicate the sorts of tax rate graphs that would apply to hourly tax averaging. Prior to the graphs, however, I will explain the limits on progressivity and indicate why it is possible to have much higher marginal and average tax rates when taxing on an hourly-average basis. The description of economic matters is brief here since I will discuss the economic issues surrounding hourly averaging in more detail towards the end of chapter three.

When describing the features of a good tax system, I explained it is irrational for effective marginal and participatory tax rates to reach 100%. This is the extreme limit on tax progressivity, but in some cases it may be that 80% or 90% tax rates would also have such damaging effects on incentives—and thereby economic activity and growth—which would render them unattractive. A further worry is that some products would be rendered extremely expensive—or unavailable—due the high tax rates on their producers.[31] Some people may not be able to undertake their previous form of work or purchase their preferred products as a result of higher taxation. This would interfere with their ability to carry out their plans.

Hourly-averaging should enable much higher tax rates before the above-mentioned effects become problematic. This means that it should be possible for tax rates to reach the highest possible level; up to 99.99% on those who have an incredibly high hourly income. This does not create troubling disincentives because those very few with such a high income will have received it through windfalls or on rents received.[32] Taxing the extremely fortunate at this level is attractive, as it generates large revenues that can be used to subsidise the incomes of the less fortunate without causing economic damage.

I will not specify particular tax rates that should be applied, since these depend on the particular facts of the society in question. However, I will present some lifetime hourly tax rate graphs that would be attractive.[33] These graphs obey certain constraints. The first constraint is that *the tax rate should always rise.*[34] Second, *every income point must have one and only one tax rate.*[35] The third and final constraint is that *the graph should never be vertical nor reach 100%.*[36] Accordingly, all graphs rise up to a 99.99% tax rate which they should never exceed. Figures 1.3 and 1.4 are curved, while 1.5 and 1.6 have several straight lines. Figures 1.5 and 1.7 have a kink which may make them more attractive as they provide fewer disincentives for those with high ability to practice their abilities. My hypothesis is that the slightly more complicated graph in figure 1.7 may prove to be the most attractive.

Figure 1.3: Smooth curve (logarithmic)

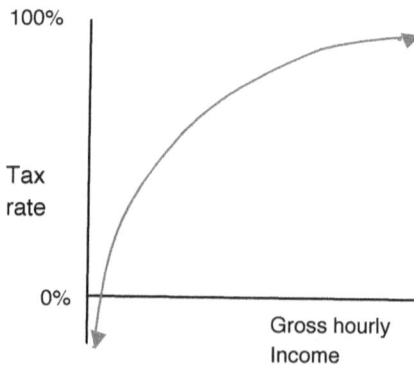

Figure 1.4: Smooth graph with kink

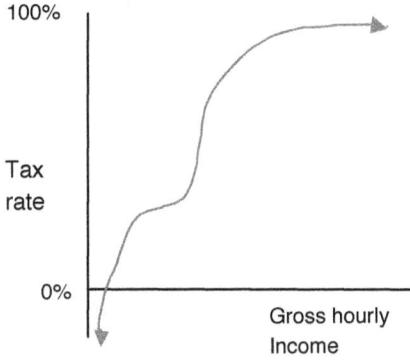

Figure 1.5: Straight-line graph with kink

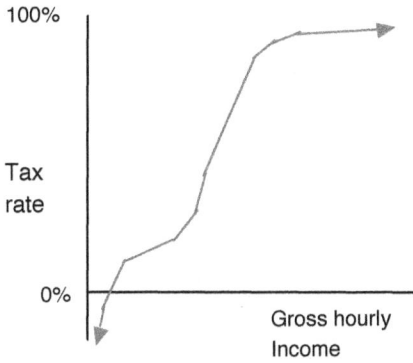

Figure 1.6: Straight-line graph

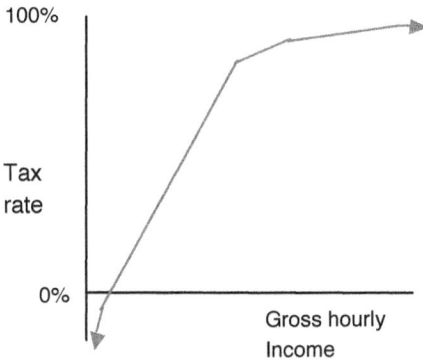

Figure 1.7: Curved graph with kink around 0% tax point

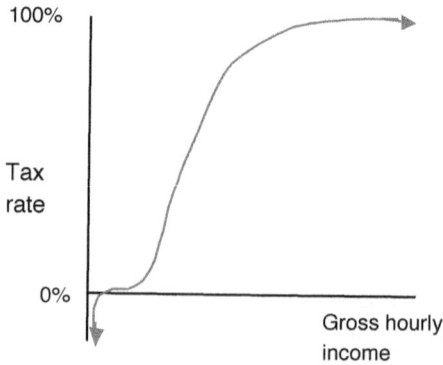

As I have indicated, net income will always rise with gross income, as shown in the following graph. This plots gross income against net income. Where there is a kink in the graph, this will cause a faster rise in the kinked region. These points are illustrated in figures 1.7 and 1.8.

Figure 1.8: Net income always rises when gross income does

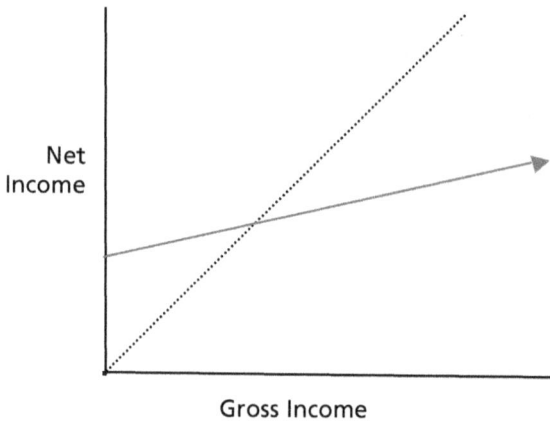

Figure 1.9: Net income increases with kinked graph

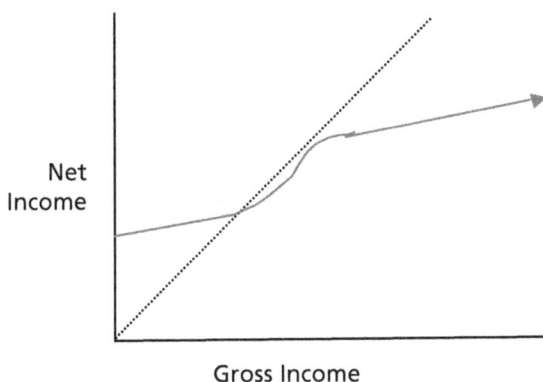

I emphasise that these graphs apply to the lifetime average gross-hourly-income, which smooths out changes in people's incomes. This smoothing occurs because people will usually move very slowly along the graph over time.[37] It is also important to remember that marginal tax rates do not work in the same way with hourly-averaging as with any other tax system. This is because the decision to work an additional hour will have a *reducing* effect on the person's lifetime tax rate. With other systems, the individual's marginal tax rate simply applies on their *next hour*[38] *worked* and so the headline marginal tax rate is much more important.

Conclusion

In this chapter I have explained lifetime averaging. The familiar kind of lifetime averaging is time passed based, but the subject of this book is hourly-based averaging. This is done with hour credits, which I will discuss in more detail in the following chapter. In this chapter I explained how to calculate tax rates and current taxpayer liabilities within an hourly average system. I provided some examples to illustrate the working of the system. In the final two sections I indicated the sorts of subsidy (negative tax) and (positive) tax rate graphs that could be utilised in a progressive hourly averaging system. These calculations can be undertaken instantaneously with modern computer systems. Furthermore, even though hourly averaging is more complex than other forms of taxation, taxpayers would find it straightforward to anticipate their future net income based on their knowledge of their tax rate and/or the worth that an hour credit will have to them.

CHAPTER TWO

HOUR CREDITS

HOUR CREDITS are a crucial element of hourly averaging. In this chapter I will explain what they are and the reasons for which they would be given to people. The primary reason for which people should receive an hour credit is that they have performed an hour of work for a registered employer, as I indicated in the first chapter. However, many of the sections of this chapter present further possible reasons for people to receive hour credits. The first is that those with disabilities, that would affect their ability to work, should receive additional hour credits. A second reason for people to receive additional hour credits is because they are involuntarily unemployed. I will present a scheme which would provide hour credits for job-seeking, training, and community work to those who undertake these activities. I refer to this as a guaranteed work programme. I also suggest that two further categories of work should count as hour credit worthy activities. These are hour credits for students and also hour credits for those who provide care.

In the later parts of the chapter I discuss other points relating to hour credits. The first is that I would propose setting a maximum number of hour credits that taxpayers could receive in a given period. The second point is that hour credits enable a novel and effective form of punishment: hour credit fines. The third issue I engage with arises given that some people may wish to remove themselves from the economy. I explain that this would be broadly possible in an economic system featuring hour credits.

Source and nature of hour credits

I will begin by making clear some of the basic features of hour credits. The first point to explain is the *source* of hour credits. It should have been clear from the discussion in the previous chapter that the primary source of hour credits would be employers. This additional responsibility for employers—and their personnel managers—would be an extremely important community role. Corporations and smaller businesses already play an important role in society, of course, and already receive social benefits. They are legal fictions and yet they receive the benefits of the right to trade enabled by their legal personhood and limited liability. There is no reason not to require these entities to provide whatever information is required in order to best meet the public duties they obtain in exchange for these benefits.[39]

In order to be able to confer hour credits, therefore, employers would need to meet strict criteria. These would include submitting their full financial reports, proving regularly that the company is a viable business which has sufficient funds to trade, submitting to regular comprehensive audits and enabling civil servants to undertake unannounced inspections. It is necessary to impose strict constraints on employers since the power to confer hour credits is a very valuable one, and the authorities would need to ensure that this power is not abused. I will therefore devote a chapter—chapter seven—to hour credit fraud in order to discuss the issue in greater detail.

Institutions and enterprises which employ people are not the only ones which should have the right to confer hour credits. I will explain that hour credits should be conferred on those with severe disabilities and on those who are involuntarily unemployed. I will also discuss the possibility of conferring additional hour credits to those who undertake caring responsibilities and to students. In the following sections I will discuss these sources of *additional hour credits*.

The second point to clarify is the *nature* of hour credits. Hour credits would not take any physical form but would take a virtual form on the tax authority computer system.[40] They would be credited by registered legal entities (such as approved managers of registered employers), as I have indicated. The tax authority would use these credits to calculate taxation and net income figures. Hour credits would not be transferrable in any way and therefore, although the credits would have significant monetary value to their recipients, they would not be a form of currency.

Hour credits for the disabled

Those with disabilities sometimes face discrimination in employment decisions as well as in other areas of life. Hopefully any remnants of such discrimination will disappear in the near future. However, notwithstanding such discrimination, many people with disabilities would still face greater economic disadvantages than others. The most extreme form of economic disadvantage will fall on those disabled persons who are unable to perform productive work in the marketplace. Given the importance of hour credits in an hour-credit-based tax system, it would be necessary to provide those who have disabilities with hour credits in order to ensure that their tax rate is not unduly affected. This is particularly important where a comprehensive tax base is applied, as I assumed in the examples in the previous chapter and will argue for in chapter four. Without hour credits, the severely disabled will not be able to obtain any income.

Not all people with disabilities are entirely unable to work, of course. Some disabled people will be able to work but still face disadvantages outside work. I propose that some disabled workers should receive additional hour credits to compensate them for their disabilities. One way to think about hour credits is that they should indicate the amount of leisure-time that individuals have. Yet some people with disabilities will have to spend their 'leisure-time' preparing for work in ways that those without any disabilities do not. I therefore propose that people with disabilities, which renders undertaking paid work more time-consuming for them than it is for others, should be able to receive additional hour credits to compensate them for this disadvantage.

The hour credits suggested should be conferred in *addition* to the provision of any other aids or caring support that is provided to the disabled. However, the level of additional hour credits provided to the disabled should of course be calculated with consideration of the assistance received. So, imagine someone who will need to spend several hours in the morning to get ready for work. However, their local government funds a carer to assist them, meaning that the process takes little more than it would for other workers. In this case, there is no need to provide additional hour credits, since the disabled person does not face a relative time deficit.

Involuntary unemployment and the guaranteed work programme

It is crucial to provide additional hour credits to those who cannot work because they have a disability. However, there are sometimes people who are perfectly capable of work but cannot find any: the *involuntarily unemployed*. It is just as important to ensure that such individuals have access to hour credits. I therefore suggest that the government should utilise hour credits as part of a *guaranteed work programme*.[41] Another way to put this is that the government, via local government projects, should be the *employer of last resort*.

Advanced countries provide income assistance to those who are able to convince the authorities that they are searching for work but have not obtained any. In the UK, for example, this is currently referred to as a "jobseeker's allowance." Jobseekers sometimes have to undertake training and do work experience as part of their contract with the authorities, administered in each locality by a "jobcentre." I would suggest that in an economic system with hour credits it would be beneficial to combine the unemployment system and tax system. However, when combining these together, it would become even more pressing to go further than most programmes currently do.

Instead of requiring jobseekers to undertake occasional training and projects, a guaranteed work programme would attempt to ensure that jobseekers have some useful activity on which to engage. In exchange for this activity the jobseeker would obtain valuable hour credits. The useful activities would either be designed to help jobseekers secure a paid job in the future or it would provide some benefit to the local community. My suggestion would be for each local government to have a job and training programme with a number of permanent staff to administer the programme. These staff will organise training and local job schemes.

The training would be designed to help jobseekers find work in their local economy, providing them with new skills and capabilities. This could be provided by a mixture of internal trainers and outside professionals. The programme would work with potential employers to ensure that jobseekers are able to meet future demand for skills in their area. So, for example, a company considering opening a new facility might ask the job programme to prepare a certain number of staff for the work that they are likely to require.[42] The training could also enable people to undertake jobs found by the programme, of the sort I will describe shortly.

As well as assisting jobseekers in obtaining valuable skills and encouraging new employers to their local area, the job programme would arrange for jobseekers to do work in their local community. There are an abundance of schemes that could be devised to improve the local area or the quality of life of local residents. For example, clearing and cleaning public land and structures. There will also be many services that would be useful to local institutions such as assistance in schools, libraries, hospitals, hospices, care homes, and correctional facilities. These schemes would improve the quality of life, or education, of those who would benefit from additional assistance. Increasing the number of such schemes might involve a greater amount of bureaucracy in order to ensure that all those involved are partaking appropriately. However, on larger projects, it would be possible to appoint some jobseekers as overseers on the schemes. These would be given the responsibility of ensuring that all the people involved are performing the required work in order to obtain the hour credits. Those who shirk on such schemes would simply not receive the full amount of hour credits.

One point I would stress at this stage is that the job programme should not displace paid labour. This is important since those on a job scheme may have to leave at any time if they secure full employment elsewhere. It would not be advisable, therefore, for employers to rely on such labour to provide their goods and services. Furthermore, if profit-making businesses are able to obtain labour for free, it would give them an inappropriate advantage in the marketplace. An exception may be possible where businesses require a short term labour force and are willing to pay the job guarantee programme rather than temporarily employ the workers directly. Furthermore, businesses should be able to provide training under the auspices of the programme if they provide the trainer and promise to hire a certain number of those who pass the training.

Unemployment is not only a very costly waste to society, but it is also often bad for the long-term unemployed. It is bad for people's self-esteem that they are unable to contribute to their society,[43] and people can lose the habit of work as a result of long periods of unemployment. A guaranteed work programme would do more to reduce these harms than the more limited programmes currently employed.

The downside of the more extensive guaranteed job programme is that it would be more costly to administer. However, if hour credits play an important role in lifetime taxation calculations, then it is crucial to offer people the chance to obtain these *throughout* their working lives. Furthermore, despite the increased baseline costs of administering a more extensive programme, the overall cost may not be that large. One reason is that the programme may reduce the long-term costs to society of unemployment in lost work, less productive workers, drug-taking, and crime. A second reason is that the programme would be much more effective at screening out those who simply do not wish to work and who can game the limited system in order to obtain an additional income. This would reduce costs since fewer people would be recipients of assistance. Third, the existence of an earnings subsidy—the negative tax rates on low average gross income—instead of the imposition of a minimum wage, should also massively reduce the quantity of involuntary unemployment. It would mean employers can offer people very low pay and the worker will still receive a reasonable income. If an employer has a relatively attractive form of work then it would be able to hire workers at low wages and little cost, since it can also confer hour credits at little cost to itself.

Additional hour credits: Students and carers

I have argued that it would be necessary to provide hour credits for those with disabilities and involuntary unemployment. In this section I will suggest two further types of work that should be candidates for additional hour credits under an hour credit system; for *students and carers.*

Innumerable advantages follow from a more educated society. For one thing, education often brings greater economic productivity. However, knowledge is also an end in itself, and the cultural capital of a society is of immense value. In addition, a more educated society should have a better quality of democratic debate. Not providing hour credits to students would create a significant disincentive for adults to undertake any further education. This is because hour credits have great value in the short term, but will also bring down tax rates for the rest of the taxpayer's life. For example, a medical doctor will have to study for several years before earning a premium as a result of her skills. If she were not provided with hour credits for her studies then she would have a very high tax rate as a result of her high income as well as missing out on an income for the period of her study. This would make professions involving long periods of study and training very financially unattractive.

In the following section I will discuss maximum hour credits, and will suggest a lower weekly or monthly maximum for those who work without pay, such as students, and those on the guaranteed job programme. However, full-time students should receive hour credits via their college or university in recognition of their studies. Continued receipt of the credits should depend upon the completion of the various parts of longer courses. All courses offered by approved colleges and universities should qualify if they meet the required standards of rigour.

There should be some restrictions in place in order to avoid the opportunity for leisure-lovers with a love and talent for education to study for their entire adult lives and thus avoid productive work or the application of their knowledge. This would be possible where students could obtain an income via their hour credits which would cover their living costs and also the costs of their course. It should be possible to block such activities easily enough. One option is to directly limit hour credits for each taxpayer for only one undergraduate degree. Alternatively, this can be achieved by proxy by making hour credits conditional on the provision of public funding or loan, and payment of any fees where such funding is offered only for those who do not already have a degree. For postgraduate courses, the payment of fees or the existence of funding for the student could be used as measures of the appropriateness of hour credits for the student in question.

The second group of people who should be candidates for additional hour credits are carers. Some people take on caring responsibilities for their relatives and thereby save their society huge amounts of resources.[44] In most cases it is better for all parties involved if a loved one undertakes caring responsibilities. This is because the carer will better know the needs and desires of their loved ones and because most people would prefer to be cared for by someone they know if this was not too costly for them.

As well as hour credits for those who care for disabled individuals, it might be advisable to provide additional hour credits to those who look after infants, which could replace maternity and paternity payments. Although people are responsible for bearing children,[45] while people do not choose to have disabled relatives and friends, the benefits of providing care to children at a young age may be so great that society should make sure this care is provided.

Carers accept great sacrifices when caring for their loved ones, even if they are perfectly willing to bear such costs without compensation. Carers will have less time for jobs and careers, and if they undertake the paid work they would have done otherwise then their caring responsibilities will have a massive impact upon their leisure time. Carers, then, face a life with less income or leisure (or both) as a result of the misfortune of having a disabled relative or friend. Of course women currently undertake the vast majority of such caring responsibilities, and this is a further cause of the relative economic disadvantage that many women face.

I therefore propose that those who look after disabled loved ones should receive additional hour credits corresponding to the amount of time that professional carers would spend caring for someone with the needs of those whom they support. It should be calculated on the basis of the time that professionals would spend caring for someone with those needs, since it would be expensive to accurately monitor how long each carer actually spends. Furthermore, people should not receive additional compensation for their relative lack of efficiency at the role. After all, the hour credits correspond to the cost savings for the society given that the caring avoids the need for society to provide professional care for those who need it. The need for such care would be determined by local government workers and social workers in association with medical doctors.

Maximum hour credits

As I have hinted above, I think it would be advisable to cap the number of hour credits that taxpayers can obtain in a given period. I would suggest that there should be two different maximums. One should apply to the hour credits that a taxpayer can obtain from *paid* employment in a given period, such as a week. The limit could be set at something like 42 or 45 hours a week. It would be possible for people to work more hours than this if they wished to; the limit would merely apply to the number of *hour credits* that someone could obtain. A major advantage of limiting hour credits is that it would reduce the scope for people to commit hour credit fraud, an issue I will discuss in much greater detail in chapter seven.

Another advantage of placing a maximum limit on hour credits is that it would reduce the scope for the proliferation of a long-hours culture. Some workplaces generate an arms race whereby staff feel they have to stay longer and longer in order to prove their dedication to their work.[46] In other work-places pressure may simply be placed upon workers to perform overtime in order to keep their jobs. Setting a limit on hour credits would give workers much greater power in standing up to employers. Employers would only be able to offer them a limited number of hour credits as part of their compensation, so any additional overtime workers perform beyond the maximum would be much less remunerative than their contracted work. Workers could work longer if they wished, for example if they happen to prefer their job to any other leisure activity, but they would be in a stronger position to stand up to unreasonable or exploitative employers. Not only would an hour credit maximum benefit most workers, it would also benefit society as a whole. After all, workers will be much less productive if they have not had adequate rest and so working time limits can be economically beneficial.[47]

I would suggest that a lower maximum should apply for *unpaid* or *additional* hour credits. So a maximum of something like 35 hours a week might be applied to those who receive each kind of additional hour credit. This would apply even if students are expected to work more hours than this as part of their courses. This restriction is advisable in order to ensure that people have a greater incentive to undertake mainstream employment rather than these alternatives.

Of course, some people may receive additional hour credits *as well* as hour credits from employment. So a student may also have a part-time job in addition to full-time study, and a part-time carer may also have a job with full-time hours. In this case, a *cumulative* maximum could be applied either at the level of the employment maximum or perhaps a slightly higher level. Whether or not to have a higher cumulative maximum than the standard maximum would depend upon the incentive effects this would create.

Hour credit fines

I have so far discussed the source and nature of hour credits and what rules should apply to them. In this section I will briefly mention an additional useful policy that is available in a society with an hour-credit-based tax system. This is that it would become possible to apply what might be called *hour credit fines* or *hour debits*. This form of punishment could take the place of fines, community service, and prison for those who have committed non-violent crimes. The net cost of the fine for the delinquent taxpayer will be automatically linked to her economic situation, and a fine of x number of credits will therefore have a suitably proportionate effect on all taxpayers despite the differing cost to their net income. This therefore avoids the need for judges to take account of the economic situation of those facing punishment.

Hour credit fines could be applied by judges when sentencing offenders. Imagine that a judge fines someone 150 hour credits for committing fraud. Such fines could be applied either immediately or they could be applied over a long period into the future. If the taxpayer has previous hour credits removed from his account then this will increase his lifetime tax rate. As a result, since the individual will have therefore received too much lifetime net income, his account would be in deficit. If the taxpayer has sufficient money, or owns assets which could be sold, then this *immediate application* approach might be preferable.

However, some people may not be able to pay such a bill up front. In this case the *future application* approach would be useful. This would be to apply a debit to future weekly (or monthly) hour credits at a rate of, say, 5 per week (or 21 per month) until the fine were paid-off. In most cases this future debiting would be more appropriate. However, it might be necessary to utilise an immediate fine on some people without assets readily available to pay off their immediate debt. This would apply to those nearing the end of their working life or those who are already paying substantial hour debits for past crimes.[48]

There are several advantages to hour credit fines over alternative forms of punishment. Prison is extremely expensive and unnecessary for those who pose no physical risk to others. Community service would also be more expensive to administer than simply setting up a regular hour debit on the tax computer system. It would take an administrator a matter of seconds to apply such a rule. A further advantage is that workers could continue to perform a useful form of work, which will benefit the community anyway. The recipient of the fine will pay a higher tax rate than they would have if they had not committed the transgression, and also more than a fellow citizen with an otherwise similar economic situation. This means that those who have committed crimes against their community can be said to provide more tax revenue by way of compensation.

Life without hour credits in an hour credit society

I have emphasised that hour credits are extremely important in a society in which they play a role in tax calculations, and this role is even more important when such calculations apply to a comprehensive tax base. It was for this reason that I argued it is so important to ensure that additional hour credits are available to the disabled and involuntarily unemployed. However, some people may think that hour credits play such an important role in the system that the system would be oppressive. Some people may think that modern society is unacceptable and wish not to partake in it. In this section I will therefore discuss the prospects of living a life without working and earning hour credits in an hour credit society. I will offer two examples which show that it would be possible to live in an hour credit society without hour credits and without breaking the law. These examples refer to difficult and precarious lifestyles; however, they show the possibility of a life without hour credits.

The first example of a life without hour credits is that of living on the streets and begging. A comprehensive tax base, such as the acquired income tax base which I will suggest in chapter four, would disallow the receipt of all forms of resources to those without hour credits. However, even the most comprehensive approach I suggest would still exclude the receipt of gifts of low value as income (or consumption) within the comprehensive tax base. Since it would be possible for beggars to survive on numerous gifts of low value from numerous different people, these gifts would not be taxable and they would be able to live off any generosity they could obtain. Similarly, people may be able to survive on the detritus of a modern society; sadly, many impoverished people around the world already live in such a way due to a lack of choice. Obtaining food and other resources from begging, searching rubbish, or both would be one way to survive without hour credits.

A second example will perhaps appear nobler. This is the life of a subsistence farmer, fisher, or beachcomber. There may be tracts of marginal land that would be available to purchase for little money, and those who wished to purchase them would not need very many hour credits in order to save up to buy them. Once purchased, the smallholder could live on the produce of their land without having to pay any tax. As long as they did not engage economically with the rest of society their consumption would not fall under the remit of even a comprehensive tax base.

These two examples show that it would be possible to live a life without obtaining hour credits, though that life would no doubt be a precarious and dangerous one. Some may feel that these options are unfair and that society should provide dissidents with more than this. However, I do not see the force of such a claim. Anyone who does not wish to engage with, nor contribute to, a modern society does not have much of a claim for a subsidy from the society they reject. People have no cause to seek to overthrow a legitimate society and economic system, and the progressive hour credit society would be more than merely legitimate, it would be fully economically just.[49] Nevertheless, in this section I have shown that any person who did feel that they could not engage economically with such a society would have at least two options open to them.

Conclusion

Hour credits play a crucial role in hourly averaging, and in this chapter I have clarified their nature and how taxpayers would obtain them. They would obtain hour credits on their tax account from several sources, the main source being that of paid employment by a registered employer. In addition, I have suggested that hour credits should be available to the disabled, those who perform what is required of them by a guaranteed job scheme, students, and carers. I suggested that it would be advisable to place a maximum limit on hour credits, and that it would be possible to utilise hour credit fines in place of other forms of punishment. In the final section I outlined how it would be possible for someone to live a life without hour credits in a society in which hour credits are generally crucial for the receipt of net income.

CHAPTER THREE

WHY INTRODUCE HOURLY AVERAGING?

IN THIS CHAPTER I will explain why hourly averaging is superior to both the current tax system and any other alternative that has been proposed. In order to do this I will consider how it fares according to the principles of a good tax system I set out in the introduction. In the first section I will outline these principles and discuss some of the issues. Hourly averaging has a clear advantage on the issues of distributive justice and economic motivation, so I will present several sections which explain these issues separately.

Principles of taxation

In the introduction I described four features of a good tax and benefit system. I will discuss the first and fourth of these in greater detail in the remainder of this chapter, since there is much to say on these issues. These are that a good tax system will distribute resources appropriately, and that the system should not have detrimental economic effects. I will focus in this section on the second and third features.

The second feature I described was that the tax system should not restrict people in living their lives. Some people would be much better off with an annual system than a progressive hourly one, as I will describe in the following section. However, this difference does not count as a restriction on the lives of these people in any morally troubling way. Their complaint is just that they have to pay tax and would be better off if they had to pay less, but this is true of everyone—everyone would be better off if they paid less in tax and received more in compensation. The relevant issue is that hourly averaging does not force anyone to undertake certain forms of work.

With hourly averaging, those with certain aptitudes are not forced to use them. People will have to do *some* work in their lives in order to obtain what they need to survive (through their need to obtain hour credits in order to receive net income). However, the vast majority of people in the history of humanity have needed to work in order to survive, and so this requirement cannot be described as a serious restriction on people living their lives. I will discuss the tax base later on—in chapter four—where I will make clear that the proposal need not fall foul of the worry that people will have to sell their property prematurely.

The third feature of a good tax system was that the system should be convenient to taxpayers, and stable. As I said in the introduction, I think that the judicious use of IT systems can render hourly averaging a convenient system for taxpayers. If taxpayers wish to model their future tax liabilities and net income they should be able to do so using an app or online tax account. This would utilise the individual's past records and combine them with their projections of the future. So a taxpayer considering a new job, or a change to the number of hours they work, could model their options in order to see what their net income would be in each scenario. In practice, of course, taxpayers can make reasonable guesstimates of their future income; people's hourly net income will not usually change rapidly. This means that taxpayers will know each additional hour credit they obtain will give them £x of net income and each pound of gross income will correspond to a particular amount of net income.

The other aspect of convenience is that people should be able to pay their taxes in a convenient manner. However, I propose that employers and/or financial institutions should undertake the majority of tax collection directly and automatically. Taxpayers would merely need to check that their hour credits and income records were correct. Again, this can be done through their online tax account, though telephone and other methods of interaction should be available to them as well.

This may lead us to a different worry, that the system is convenient for individual taxpayers at the expense of huge inconvenience for employers. The worry here is that businesses would be overburdened by the requirements of reporting hours worked and withholding taxation. However, businesses currently withhold taxes in the UK and most developed countries. The additional burden would therefore be that employers would have to report the number of hours that their workers have worked. However, with modern IT interfaces this should not be a time consuming task for managers. After all, they would have this information on their staff anyway.

Who is better-off and who is worse-off with hourly averaging?

When considering a new taxation proposal an important question to ask is who would be better-off and worse-off as a result. When answering this question, it is necessary to consider what the alternative is, against which we compare the proposal. It is not fair to compare a proposal to the best elements of all the alternatives, and so I will mostly compare the system to a slightly progressive annual taxation and benefit system of the sort which exists in more economically developed countries like the USA, Canada, France, and the UK.

If everyone would be better-off then of course the case for progressive hourly averaging is simple, and there is one sense in which everyone is better-off. This is that *everyone* is better-off if they live in a just and fair society. It is simply better to live in a just society than an unjust one. Furthermore, there are burdens on people living in an unjust society—the pain of living in such a society, and the time and energy that they are duty-bound to spend in attempting to transform their society into a just one. However, notwithstanding this point about justice, it is certainly the case that some people would find themselves much materially worse-off with hourly averaging. I will briefly outline who can expect to be better and worse-off.

It is useful to classify people in order to answer the question of this section. People have different levels of fortune and different preferences. People might be more or less fortunate in their native abilities and their family background. Concerning their preferences, people may prefer work over leisure or *vice versa*. They may prefer work because they are keen on obtaining resources (they are consumption-lovers) or because they value their work due to their work-ethic, desire to contribute to society, or simply because they enjoy their work more than other uses of their time.

Broadly speaking, the less fortunate would be better-off with hourly averaging and the more fortunate would be worse-off than they would be otherwise. The proposal would more effectively tax the more fortunate and provide more targeted subsidies to the less fortunate, as I will describe in later sections of this chapter. One form of fortune is the gifts and inheritances that people receive—their social fortune. If people are taxed comprehensively, as I will suggest in the following chapter, then those who are fortunate in the wealth they obtain from their relatives will have a higher average hourly gross income. They will then be taxed at a higher rate than they would otherwise be. This will add more resources into the pot for redistribution, meaning that more resources will go to those who have not benefitted from good social fortune.

The main consequence of hourly averaging is to transfer income from those who earn large amounts per-hour to those who earn less per-hour. In many cases, this will mean that high-earners will be worse-off with the introduction of hourly averaging. However, in some cases it may be necessary to pay people in certain jobs a particular premium over the average wage in order to provide them with a net income sufficient to incentivise them to undertake the work. In these cases, the increased taxation may be passed on to the consumers of the products and services in question. Those who pay for these services would therefore be worse-off, though in most cases these costs would be spread between numerous consumers and would not therefore fall particularly hard on any one group or individual.

It may appear that those I refer to as leisure-lovers will be much worse-off with hourly averaging. In many cases, this will no doubt be true. Leisure-lovers who would otherwise benefit from social fortune would be less able to live a life of leisure if gifts were included in the tax base I propose in chapter four. Those with high hourly gross earnings who work part-time—such as Bertrand in chapter one—would also be worse-off with hourly averaging; with progressive annual taxation they can avoid higher tax rates due to their reasonably low annual income. The more fortunate leisure-lovers would therefore be better-off without hourly averaging. However, many of the less fortunate leisure-lovers would be better-off with hourly averaging. The additional wage subsidy enabled by hourly averaging may allow these leisure-lovers to afford to work fewer hours.

If my proposal to include a guaranteed work scheme were also included as part of the scheme, this would also make some leisure-lovers worse-off while improving the situation for the vast majority of low-earners. Some leisure-lovers may currently find ways to game the unemployment benefit system in order to avoid working consistently. The programme would remove these means to achieve both income and leisure. The guaranteed work scheme would benefit regular workers by improving their bargaining position with regard to employers, both when they are in-work and applying for work. The existence of a reasonably-paid alternative to work in the marketplace would enable workers to drive a better deal for themselves and would remove the fear of destitution that workers would face when considering whether to stand up to unreasonable employers.

As should be clear, then, the group that would benefit the most from hourly averaging are those who desire to work or consume a lot but who cannot secure a high wage when doing so. These workers will have their income subsidised to the greatest extent by hourly averaging and would be the main beneficiaries. In addition, if hour credits are provided for those who care for others, as I have suggested, then this is another group of people who would be much better under hourly averaging. Given that the vast majority of carers are women at the present time, the system would therefore make this group of less fortunate women much better-off.

Finally, I would note that the system I propose should make it much harder for criminals to operate, meaning that they will be much worse-off. This is because they would have to have greater interaction with the tax authority due to their need to give and receive hour credits. As a result, criminal enterprises would have to go to greater lengths to cover their activities, and in many cases would no doubt find it impossible to cover their tracks—particularly if my comprehensive taxation proposal from chapter four were introduced as well. The requirement for greater international integration and co-operation I describe in chapter eight would make it much harder for the international super-rich to avoid taxation as well.

I have presented the above list without very much commentary. However, I doubt many readers will be concerned for those who would be worse-off under hourly averaging, and will be quite pleased to see the groups who would benefit. This is because the most fortunate would have to pay more in taxation, while less fortunate people will benefit more. This was the first feature of a good taxation system that I described in the introduction. In the following section I will explain how the system is extremely effective at redistributing the resources that follow from fortune and why it is therefore superior to the current system—and other proposals—with regard to redistribution. In the subsequent section I will explain why the system allows this redistribution without the usual economic disincentives.

Effective redistribution

I have claimed that hourly averaging does a better job of redistributing from the fortunate to the less fortunate. In this section I will recap why that is the case, particularly when comparing to alternative proposals. I will continue to compare the taxation implications to the current system of annual progressive taxation. However, hourly averaging is also a form of redistribution to the less fortunate, and so in this section I will compare it to its rivals; the minimum wage, basic income, and alternative methods of subsidising income. In essence, hourly averaging is much better at determining people's relative fortune than its rivals. This becomes clearer when focussing on the two issues separately.

Lifetime hourly averaging is superior to *annual* taxation because it takes both a longer and a shorter timeframe. By taking account of lifetime income, it is possible to differentiate between people who have had better fortune overall from those with temporary good fortune. Indeed, even in 1939 Vickrey wrote that it had long been recognised that progressive annual taxation is unfair to those whose income fluctuates.[50] In their high-income years they will pay very high rates of tax, despite the fact that they do not earn particularly much overall.

The classic example is that of an author who has occasional sales success.[51] However, the point also applies to those who spend a long time working their way up to position where they can obtain high pay or a return on their company. Such individuals may not have a particularly large lifetime income, but in their later years they will have a large annual income, and a progressive annual tax would tax such individuals at a high-rate. Annual taxation cannot differentiate those who have worked their way up to a large annual income, or those who earn incomes that are split between multiple years, from those who are simply fortunate and thereby able to earn money more easily than the other members of their society.

Lifetime hourly averaging would also be useful for those who face a large drop in income even if they are not in the subsidy region. Another way to put this is that it *smooths* out changes in income and fortune. So rather than face an immediate drop in net income when gross income falls, a worker's average would gradually move down their tax graph towards the lower-tax and subsidy regions. As a result, they would effectively receive back the tax they previously paid as their lifetime tax rate would become more and more favourable. This smoothing effect is attractive as it means that people have an incentive to earn larger amounts in the first place (as workers know they can receive the tax back in the future if their fortune changes) and also because a sudden change in financial circumstances can have a big impact upon someone's life. Income-smoothing would mitigate against the latter worry by allowing people to gradually adjust their lifestyle to their new gross income.

Extending the horizon of taxation from a year to a lifetime should therefore enable a fairer and more progressive tax system. However, there are even greater benefits to reducing the denominator of the averaging equation from a year to an hour. Hourly wages are simply a much better indicator of someone's fortune in the job market rather than annual income. If someone has earned a high average hourly income across their working life then they are clearly very capable of earning money—they are more fortunate in this regard—and should accordingly be taxed at a higher rate than those who find it harder to earn money.

The advantage of hourly averaging with regard to determining levels of economic fortune can be illustrated by considering the four example individuals from chapter one.[22] Angela and Bertrand were the more economically fortunate individuals, while Cassandra and Derek were less fortunate. However, while this translates readily to gross *hourly* average, it is not clear when considering lifetime income alone. Cassandra and Bertrand then seem to be in a similar position. This makes subsidies for the less economically fortunate much more complicated. Consider the tax and subsidy options available when focussing on *annual income alone.*

One option is to tax Angela the same amount as would be done under hourly averaging and to subsidise the other three. The problem with this is that there will be less money available for Derek, meaning that he will have to work more hours. However, if the subsidy is instead focussed on very low-earners, such as Derek, then this will exclude assistance for Cassandra. Furthermore, Bertrand may drop his hours in order to qualify for this subsidy as well, meaning that Derek will still have to share the subsidy with Bertrand. The alternative is to tax Angela even more on the basis that Bertrand—despite being economically fortunate—is going to obtain some of the subsidy. However, increasing taxation on Angela may result in her working less, since the advantage to her of working longer is minimal. This would further reduce the revenue available to assist Derek and Cassandra. Furthermore, the loss of work throughout the economy may damage economic growth. Alternatively, Angela may be so desperate for any extra revenue that she will continue to work just as hard. In this case, the economic consequences would not be as dire. However, it is still the case that Angela, Cassandra, and Derek would all prefer the hourly averaging system, given that Bertrand does so well out of the non-hourly system even though it is not intended to support high-earners such as him.

The examples I gave in the first chapter were of course highly simplified. There may be some jobs which pay extremely well but which do not require unusual natural talent or good fortune. Presumably jobs which involve unpleasant and dangerous conditions would fall into such a category, though examples are hard to think of—the best I can come up with are oil-rig workers, mercenary soldiers, deep-sea divers, and ice truckers. However, even these may involve natural abilities—to be less troubled by such difficult environments for example— and those who do such jobs might therefore be considered to have special talents. If people were unwilling to do such work without a significant net pay premium then these jobs would no longer be done, if consumers were not willing to pay the tax in order to maintain the net pay premium. In some cases this would be a loss, as the worker and consumers would miss out on their preferred transaction. However, I would think that many of those undertaking such work do so for a brief period of their lives and then move on to other work. Hourly averaging allows people to intersperse such highly-paid undesirable jobs with less undesirable work to increase their overall income without having to do the unpleasant work for long periods. If this job-sharing were increased, it would simply share the burden of such work among a wider number of people in society. [52]

As I have indicated, hourly averaging is also better at redistributing towards those who are less fortunate. I will therefore take the opportunity to compare it to other means to improve the position of the less economically fortunate in society. One—rather unfashionable—option to improve the position of the less fortunate is for governments to provide certain kinds of public goods, usually those that are important for a decent standard of life, such as housing and utilities. These could be focused either at those who are considered to be badly-off or subsidised for everyone. In the latter case, the policy is a very expensive one that will not redistribute in a targeted way. However, in the former case it is still difficult to target the good effectively. After all, how easy is it for the government to determine who should be given these expensive public goods and to redirect these as people's situations change? It seems likely that the goods will be targeted at those who are badly-off at a particular point in time, but it would be difficult to later take the good from them to provide to others. In practice, then, it would seem that these subsidies would be provided to increasing numbers of people as time goes on, at increasing cost and with decreasing focus on the worst-off. It is therefore also a rather economically inefficient form of redistribution, an issue I will discuss further in the following section.

A second approach is to provide a so-called *basic income* to all those who earn below a certain amount.[53] Similar proposals have been made under the names *basic capital*,[54] *demogrant*,[55] *stakeholder grant*,[56] *minimum income*,[57] and *negative income tax*.[58] These proposals all seek to top-up the income of those with income below a certain threshold. This is good for the less economically fortunate as it gives them something on which to fall back when they have no work, and also improves their bargaining position with regard to employers. However, in order to maintain economic incentives to work, and for the scheme to be affordable, the subsidies would have to be kept low. This is compounded by a serious problem with basic income proposals; they focus support on leisure-lovers. People who are keen on leisure over working may take the opportunity to live on government income. This will increase the cost of the programme, reducing the resources available to support those with low market earnings.

A further consequence of the loss of work done by leisure-lovers is that prices are likely to increase throughout the economy due to the lower amount of work being done. As I have said, hourly averaging should improve the position of low-paid leisure-lovers by subsidising their hourly income and enabling them to work fewer hours for the same net pay. However, the basic income proposal goes too far the other way, doing *too much* for leisure-lovers and *not enough* for work-lovers with less market fortune.

The negative-tax aspect of hourly averaging is a form of earning subsidy, as I indicated in chapter one. However, there are other earnings subsidy proposals, and it is well to say something about the advantages of hourly averaging over these proposals. Several countries currently utilise earnings subsidies due the difficulties of living in such countries on low wages, for example the Working Tax Credit (WTC) in the UK and the Earned Income Tax Credit (EITC) in the USA.[59] These schemes top-up the income of families in which members work—they have income in a specified range—but still have a low income overall.

The problem with current forms of earning subsidy is, again, in their inability to target the right people. Since workers need to apply for the credit, some potential recipients will miss out due to a failure to apply despite their lack of economic fortune. These schemes also have problems with regard to leisure-lovers. They attempt to target the subsidy on those who work but have low incomes by either focussing on those with low income from earned income (EITC) or by imposing a require-ment of a particular number of hours worked each week (WTC).[60] The main problem with these non-hourly subsidies is that they cannot both support those who work long hours at low-pay and avoid paying out to leisure-lovers. This is because the schemes require thresholds at either side of the range of qualifying incomes and, in the case of WTC, hours worked. These thresholds will exclude some less fortunate people who have incomes outside the required range or who do not meet the working hour threshold. For one thing, this incentivises people to work a particular amount of hours and earn a particular amount of money even if this is otherwise less convenient to them and their employers. In addition, some leisure-lovers will be able to reduce their hours in order to qualify for the subsidy and increase their leisure. These schemes are designed to support those with low hourly incomes. However, they do so in a roundabout manner and it would be better to do this directly if it is possible to do so through hourly averaging.

Another earning subsidy shares similarities to hourly averaging but operates differently. This is Edmund Phelps' plan to subsidise employers who employ low-paid workers, on a sliding scale which tapers out as income rises.[61] As an economist, Phelps knows that payments to employers will—in the medium term at least—be passed on the low-paid workers, improving their returns to work. Phelps' conservative motivation for the policy is that he wants to increase employment for inner-city men, in order to return to the idyllic society of his youth, where fathers earned and supported mothers to stay home. He therefore limits his proposal to those who work full-time hours, despite the fact that this will exclude many less fortunate individuals (mostly women). The full-time requirement will also create a threshold effect, whereby employers and workers who would rather have part-time work will have a strong incentive to have longer hours. This restriction is therefore an unattractive one. However, notice that this full-time work requirement gets around the problem of the previous proposals; it more accurately mimics an hourly subsidy. Phelps' proposal mimics the hourly subsidy for full-time earners, but this means that it needs to take account of the hours that workers work, just as hourly averaging does. It would therefore utilise the relevant information but fail to pay out to many worthy recipients.

The final alternative policy I will consider is another with an hourly element. This is the minimum wage, which sets an hourly pay-rate below which employers may not pay. Of course this again requires the choice of a threshold. If the minimum is set too low then the policy will be ineffective. It will not benefit many workers as most would get the same pay as they would have otherwise. A high threshold, on the other hand, would either cause wages to rise or it would price many workers out of the market according to mainstream economics.[62] In reality, of course, there will be a mixture of both responses. Some jobs will be performed at higher cost to consumers or taxpayers, while other jobs will be lost to countries with cheaper labour or the products will not be offered at all. In the former case, the higher wages will be passed on to consumers in the form of higher prices. In the latter case the minimum wage will lead to unemployment and many workers being worse-off. The threshold issue is a problematic one then, and an issue that does not arise for hourly averaging, which has a sliding scale of assistance in line with the hourly lifetime average for the worker. The subsidy rate is smooth and is applied on each hour credit the worker earns.

I have mentioned that other proposals would provide support to those who are not economically unfortunate, and for the sake of fairness I should consider whether this complaint can be made against hourly averaging. I have assumed that the calculation should make no reference to the earning capacity that workers have, as endowment-based taxation would.[63] This follows from my second principle of taxation set out in the introduction. This would allow people to choose to work in less well-remunerated jobs than they would be capable of doing. Some of these perfectly capable workers may have such a low average that they receive earnings subsidies despite their relative fortune. Consider, for example, someone who could earn a lot of money as a lawyer, but who works long hours for their preferred charity for a low-wage. A challenge to hourly averaging would then be that it too would expend resources on people who are not among the unfortunate.

I have three responses to this concern. The first is that taxation should not be linked to endowment as some people have suggested; endowment taxation is unfair on those who would find themselves barred from jobs that others can take—as Dworkin puts it, this would *enslave the talented*.[64] A second response is that there is a difference between those who turn their good fortune into resources and those who merely find a job they enjoy. I do not think it is acceptable for the state to judge—and tax—people on their good fortune with regard to their so-called "happiness" or "welfare."[65] It is not right to begrudge those who do a job they enjoy and this is not an appropriate issue for distributive justice.

My third response is a practical one. One worry would be that some people will take the opportunity to earn an income from doing something that they would happily do as a full-time hobby if they could. For example, people may choose to work for zero gross pay with an hourly subsidy playing their favourite sport or working for a charity which promulgates their political or religious beliefs. Since these activities will do little for others, yet it is clear that there should be scope for some people to perform such jobs, I have suggested the imposition of a differential minimum gross hourly wage.[66] This would require such jobs to be paid at a level that will not rely upon any subsidy.

I have shown that hourly averaging is better at determining and taxing the more economically fortunate than annual and non-hourly taxation. It is also better at determining and assisting the unfortunate than its rivals. To show this I compared hourly averaging to the provision of public goods, basic income, alternative earnings subsidies, and the minimum wage. An additional advantage that hourly averaging has over all of these tax and benefit proposals is that it should be more economically efficient, the issue I will discuss next.

Economic incentives

The main advantage of hourly averaging is that it provides progressive taxation and redistribution *without* producing the disadvantages usually associated with these outcomes. In this section I will explain in greater detail why this is the case. I will begin by highlighting some of the basic features of the hourly averaging calculation I set out in chapter one. I will explain some simple ways in which the system is more economically efficient before discussing it in more technical economic terms. Finally, I will emphasise how it does a good job of taxing economic rents and windfalls.

As hourly averaging is a lifetime-based calculation there are no "threshold effects," where people have an incentive to bring forward or postpone their economic transactions in order that they fall in the lowest-tax year. These threshold effects are inefficient as they interfere with the plans that people make, and require time and effort in tax planning (i.e. considering the advantages and disadvantages of making their transactions at different times). This therefore causes inconvenience to taxpayers and has knock-on effects on transactions throughout the economy.

A second simple point is that the tax rate does not reach one hundred per cent, which means that people always have a financial incentive to obtain more resources. All systems need to avoid a one hundred per cent tax rate as it would be economic insanity to incentivise people to obtain fewer resources. It is easy to achieve this for hourly averaging since there is only one form of tax calculation and it would never produce a tax rate of one hundred per cent. There are therefore no perverse incentives; people will always gain if they earn or obtain more resources.

I began the book by explaining the problem with most forms of taxation and benefit; that they produce a disincentive for people to perform work. The third simple point is that people have a strong incentive to undertake more work, at least up to the maximum hour credit point, since they will obtain hour credits by doing so. Hour credits are highly valuable as— all else being equal—they reduce the tax rate that taxpayers face on their past and future income, as well as representing an immediate source of income to them (at the value of their present net hourly income).

I will now turn to slightly more complex points regarding the economic advantages of hourly averaging, many of which relate to the points I made when describing the features of a good tax system in the introduction. I explained that low marginal and participatory tax rates are an important feature of the tax and redistribution system, and I will now explain how this is the case with hourly averaging. Marginal tax rates are kept low due to the smooth curve of the tax rate graph; there are no sudden jumps in tax rate as a person's hourly average moves along the graph. Furthermore, hour credits effectively reduce the taxpayer's tax rate at the same time as incoming resources increase it. This means that the marginal tax rate on working decisions works differently with hourly averaging when compared to any other proposal. An extra hour credit will interact with the taxpayer's past income and will continue to interact with their future income. So even someone with a 99% tax rate would almost certainly not face a 99% tax rate when they work an additional hour; they would receive some net income as a result of their hour credit at the same time as paying a high-rate of tax on their gross income.

The extremely low participation-tax rate is probably the strongest feature of hourly averaging.[67] Since hour credits are so valuable to their recipients there is a strong incentive to participate in work. This applies to those at all points of the income and fortune spectrum. Someone with a very low gross income would benefit from the earnings subsidy on their additional hour credit, just as someone with a very high income would benefit from the additional net income that the hour credit brings. This means that people will have a strong incentive to obtain work, join the guaranteed work programme, and retire later. It is still open to people to choose to take more leisure if they can afford it—for example to take early retirement if they have saved up for it. However, hour credits create a strong incentive to work longer, which counters the effect that progressive tax rates and transfer payments are usually expected to have on workforce participation.

This point about participation relates to another important feature of hourly averaging. Since people have a strong incentive to work longer, this should result in lower prices for most consumption items when compared to a minimum wage or basic income. Basic income causes price rises by allowing leisure-lovers to remove themselves from the labour force. This would push up the price of labour and therefore the price of products to consumers. Consumers will usually pay more as a result of an effective minimum wage. The increased labour costs for labour that would have been performed below the minimum wage will usually be passed on in the price of the product. An additional downside of the minimum wage not discussed in the previous section is that these price increases will fall on those who are less fortunate as much as everyone else. A further additional point to make about the minimum wage is that it will increase pay for otherwise low-paid jobs that cannot be automated, or taken by people in countries with a lower minimum wage. Minimum wages may therefore be bad for economic efficiency as the country will import more than it would with negative hourly taxation.[68] For these reasons, hourly averaging is superior to the minimum wage.

I just mentioned that hourly averaging provides better incentives to work than the provision of a basic income would. This is because it does not produce any disincentives to work. This point also applies to the limited earnings subsidies that exist at the time of writing. These have thresholds which mean that workers have a disincentive to perform work that takes them outside of the thresholds for qualification for the scheme. As I noted in the previous section, this will distort the economic choices of workers and employers.

The final economic advantage of hourly averaging I will highlight is a multifaceted one. I explained in the introduction that the most efficient forms of taxation are those which tax windfalls and economic rents. Hourly averaging, particularly when allied with a comprehensive tax base of the kind I propose in the following chapter, should do a very good job of taxing these windfalls and rents. There are two reasons for this. The first is because people cannot swap income for leisure as they can with income-only taxation; they need to work in order to obtain the hour credits necessary to reduce their tax rate and they can only get these by working. The second reason is that hourly averaging enables much more progressive tax rates without the usual disincentive problems. Non-hourly taxation has a dilemma; raising tax rates will capture a higher proportion of windfalls and rents but will reduce people's incentives to work. This dilemma is resolved by hourly averaging since there is always an incentive to utilise rents and always an incentive to work. The highly fortunate would not have the choice to opt-out of work or income as a threat to obtain a lower tax rate.

Hourly averaging is a very economically efficient form of taxation and transfer when compared to its rival policies. It provides a counteracting work incentive through the crucial role of hour credits. This means that it produces fewer disincentives than other forms of taxation and benefit policy. As a result, it is possible to set much higher tax rates on the more economically fortunate and provide larger transfers to the less economically fortunate.

Hourly averaging and economic efficiency

I have argued that hourly averaging enables a uniquely economic efficient form of taxation of the more economically fortunate and transfer to the less fortunate. However, I will briefly anticipate some broader economic points that critics may be inclined to present against the proposal. These are that progressive hourly averaging would undermine the dynamism of capitalism and that it would cause inflation.

The argument about capitalism is that because hourly averaging subsidises wages and taxes the successful, it would suppress the dynamism that capitalism engenders. This is because it reduces the penalties of economic failure and dampens the rewards to economic success. To a degree, this is true. Those who do not have valuable skills will receive assistance from the guaranteed training and job scheme and those who sell a successful company they have built from nothing will have to pay most of their economic gains in taxation.

I accept that these factors may serve to reduce the economic incentives for some workers and company owners. However, it is important to emphasise that individuals would still have some incentive to earn more gross income, since this will always translate to a higher net income. This means that those few who are motivated *solely* by money are still going to have the incentive to earn more gross income as they would with a rival system. In reality, of course, people are motivated by many things as well as money and consumption. These alternative motivations would of course continue to apply in an hourly averaging system. Company owners and other innovators may be motivated by the power or prestige of their positions, a desire to follow through on a good idea, their natural competitiveness, a desire to serve their society or local region, or any number of other motivations. Workers might be inspired and motivated by the idea of doing a job well, of providing the goods or services to customers, they may be inspired by their managers, or—again—be motivated by a desire to serve their society.

The fear of failure aspect of capitalism would still apply to a degree. People often prefer high-ranking jobs with more creativity and freedom to low-ranking jobs, and most people would probably want to avoid the guaranteed work scheme if they could avoid it. After all, workers and capitalists would presumably need to obtain hour credits and so they would want to keep a job that would be preferable to alternatives such as the work scheme. In this sense, then, the fear-based motivation would still apply to a reasonable degree. Certainly, there would be much less far to fall with lifetime hourly averaging—indeed part of the point of the system is that the worst off are less badly off than they would be under any other system. Nevertheless, the incentives for individual workers and innovators would still exist.

A further point also helps my argument about economic dynamism under hourly averaging. The most important factor of capitalism that drives innovation and economic efficiency is in the nature of capitalist *firms*. The most important point to emphasise to those who doubt the efficiency of hourly averaging, therefore, is that firms would have to compete just as they would under other forms of capitalism and that those which fail to keep up with innovations in their industry will still fail. Firms will have to innovate to dominate their industry or even to survive. This feature of capitalism would apply just as much in an hourly averaging society.

The second economic challenge to attempts to improve the position of the economically unfortunate is that they tend to produce inflation.[69] Inflation would reduce long-term economic competitiveness and could even be self-defeating as the economically unfortunate would simply have a higher cost of living to correspond to their newly improved income. The first source of inflation would occur where the ratio of spending and saving would alter. The worst-off generally spend more of their income rather than save it; they have a higher *marginal propensity to consume*. This increased spending will push up demand for many items. The second possible source of inflation is that wages would rise due to the improved employment prospects and hence bargaining power of the low skilled. This increase in wages would be passed on to consumers in higher prices, thereby driving inflation.

The first response I would make to the inflation challenge is that, as I have mentioned previously, hourly averaging may result in a *reduction* in some prices. This is because the earning subsidy would enable a significant reduction in the minimum wage, which would enable workers to take work that they may not otherwise find worth the pay. If workers did more hours as a result of the subsidy then more of the corresponding goods or services would be offered and therefore prices would fall. There are no guarantees that this effect would occur across the board and it is unlikely that *all* prices would fall. There is no way to prove without detailed investigation whether the over-all effect of these price reductions would outweigh the effect of price rises elsewhere. The price changes, however, are likely to stabilise at a new level with some higher and some lower, without any major inflationary effects. As a result, it is much less likely that the improvements for the worst-off will come at the expense of higher prices for all, as would occur with rival proposals.

The second possible source of inflation is that a shift in income to the less well-off will increase spending and reduce saving, resulting in overconsumption and price rises. Of course, one response to highlight is that if low-earners earned more they may then save more as well. Furthermore, it is possible to add policies that will ease these pressures. The first policy is that the government could operate the guaranteed work scheme in a non-inflationary manner, by shifting the source of funding for the scheme depending on inflationary pressures. Other forms of government spending could be tied to the guaranteed job policy so that government spending rises and falls as a buffer to inflation.[70] I will suggest in chapter six that the government should take on some investment through the creation of a sovereign investment fund, and this could be used as one source of funds for the job-scheme during otherwise deflationary periods and could receive funds during inflationary periods. Another policy would be to make pension investments mandatory for all workers, which may also in the long term reduce the liability of impoverished pensioners on the more responsible members of society.[71] This policy would also reduce the extent to which low-earners will spend more in the short term. These policies would reduce the problem even if it were the case that low-earners continued to spend the same proportion of their income.

The third response to the inflation challenge is a moral one. This is that, any price rises caused by hourly averaging will only reflect the fact that prices were too low previously. The prices will have been too low because low-earners will have been underpaid as a result of their poor economic position. There is no room to complain about prices that would rise since these prices were kept low in the past by an unjust economic system. This shows that while there may or may not be some short-term inflation overall as a result of hourly averaging, this will generally be a good rather than bad thing. Furthermore, through the use of the policies suggested above the system should not cause any long-term inflation or inflationary spiral.

Conclusion

In the first section of this chapter I showed how hourly averaging need not violate the second and third features of a good taxation system. The second of these principles is that it should not overly restrict people in their quest to live their lives as they wish. This would rule out certain types of taxation, such as endowment taxation and wealth taxation, but not hourly averaging. The third principle is that the system should not be inconvenient to taxpayers, and I explained that a well-designed system which makes good use of information technology would not cause too much inconvenience.

In order to discuss the other two principles of taxation I explained how the system would affect different types of people. As it would impose higher taxes on the more economically fortunate and enable a greater amount of resources to be transferred to low-earners, it is a very efficient form of redistribution. I explained these points in greater detail in the following section; I described how hourly lifetime taxation is more effective than annual taxation, and how it allows more effective transfers to the less fortunate than rival schemes. In the final section I explained how hourly averaging meets the requirement that the tax and redistribution system should not have a deleterious effect on the economy. Hourly averaging is done through hour credits, and these incentivise people to make economically efficient decisions while allowing the greatest amount of redistribution from the more economically fortunate to the less economically fortunate.

PART II

CHAPTER FOUR

THE TAX BASE

IN THE SECOND part of this book I will provide some further details on the CLIPH-rate tax. In the first part of the book I explained hourly averaging and in chapter three presented the economic advantages of the system. Some of these advantages are enhanced when combined with a comprehensive tax base, and the choice of tax base is the first subject of discussion in the second part of the book. I will argue for comprehensive taxation over broader forms of taxation and for the acquired income tax base over other forms of comprehensive taxation. In chapter five I will provide more details on the nature of lifetime taxation. I structure this discussion by splitting a lifetime into different periods and events.

In order to calculate taxation it is necessary to decide *what* will be taxed. This is referred to as the *tax base*; the resources or transactions on which the authorities apply their calculation of tax. Many different tax bases have been applied and proposed. One option is to tax the *wealth* that people hold. This would be undertaken in a thorough and consistent manner by applying a periodic wealth tax. However, any past wealth taxes have been imposed by proxy through land value taxation or by the number of windows on houses. Alternatively, certain *kinds of transaction* or transfer could be utilised as a tax base. Historically, a common form of taxation has been import and export duties. This has been attractive to governments since it is much easier to discover and value the property passing through ports and border checkpoints. Other forms of transaction tax are sales taxes and property purchase taxes.[72]

In this chapter I will explain the tax base options that are compatible with hourly averaging, and express my preferred tax base. One option is to apply hourly averaging to the separate taxation of income from labour. However, I argue that it would be better to tax people more comprehensively. I therefore present the well-known ideals of comprehensive income (accretion) taxation and consumption taxation. Due to the problems with accretion taxation I argue that consumption taxation is the more attractive of these traditional tax bases. However, I propose that it would be best to adopt a hybrid of income and consumption taxation which I refer to as the *acquired income* tax base. I explain this tax base and how the authorities would obtain the information necessary to enforce it in a way that will make fraud very difficult.

Wage income or a comprehensive tax base?

One obvious tax base on which hourly averaging could be applied is that of *labour income*. Most countries currently tax wage income separately, and it will be clear from what I have said that hourly averaging should apply to income from labour. In this way those who have highly variable income over different years of their lives—for example because they are self-employed—will pay the same lifetime amount of tax as those who earn the same amount at a more stable rate.

It is certainly attractive to apply hourly averaging to wage income, but it is *also* very attractive to apply *lifetime* averaging to unearned income. That way the person who obtains a large windfall in one year will pay the same amount of tax over their life as another who receives the same amount through several windfalls spread out over many years. Without lifetime provisions, it is impossible to tax the highly fortunate at a higher rate without also taxing those who are not as fortunate but who obtain a sizeable windfall at one point in their life— usually people receive this upon the death of their parents.

One option is therefore to introduce lifetime taxation on each of the existing separate tax bases[73] and to apply the *hourly* element to wage income only. That is, to continue with the *broad-based* tax system that is prevalent, but to calculate these taxes differently. Broad-based tax systems are popular with states as they collect tax from the easiest and cheapest sources and are readily compatible with whatever tax rules other states have.

While it is easy to see why governments are keen on broad-based taxation, this approach does not spread the burden of taxation very fairly. Governments generally ignore potentially taxable forms of income that are difficult to discover and value, such as gifts from family. This means that some very fortunate people do not face much tax relative to their good fortune. In addition, some people who are *not* among the most fortunate will pay a relatively large amount of tax if a lot of their trans-actions are easily taxable—for example if they receive regular wages and spend much of it on consumption items. This selec-tivity of broad-based taxation means that taxation does not correspond very closely to economic fortune; some of the most economically fortunate are able to pay a relatively smaller amount in taxation than many regular (so called middle-class) taxpayers who cannot shift their income into low-tax forms.

Due to these problems, many experts have preferred *compre-hensive* tax bases. These focus on the affairs of each taxpayer[74] on the whole, rather than particular kinds of transaction. I will describe two traditional forms of comprehensive taxation in the following section and propose my own suggested hybrid of these in the remaining sections of the chapter. Before that, however, I will provide some further reasons to prefer compre-hensive taxation to add to the reasons given above.

The first reason to prefer comprehensive taxation is that it generally shuts down the possibility of *recharacterisation*. This occurs where a taxpayer can pretend that a transaction of one kind is another, lower-taxed, form of transaction. This is familiar in the case of workers being paid in company shares or perks rather than taxable income. Taxing the high-earning talented workers more in a non-comprehensive system would encourage them to receive payment in other forms.

A second reason to prefer comprehensive taxation overall is that it allows differentiation between those who are *multiply* economically fortunate and those who are fortunate in only one area, and tax them differently. To see the point consider the following four individuals, who have different levels of fortune in their family background and career prospects.

Table 4.1: Individual level of taxation

	Low Talent	High talent
Small bequest	Keiron	Laura
Large bequest	Molly	Naz

If there are separate progressive taxes on wages and bequests (say 22% and 50% in these cases) then Naz will pay the most tax (50%), then Laura and Molly (somewhere between 22% and 50%, say 36% for both) and Keiron will pay the least (22%). This is a progressive outcome. However, the point I would make is that Naz should perhaps pay a greater amount of tax than he does here, since he is benefitting from two forms of good fortune. With a broad-based tax base, it is not possible to tax Naz at a higher rate without increasing the tax on Laura and Molly. This leaves the dilemma of increasing the tax on people who are not among the most fortunate overall or having fewer resources available to reduce the tax on Keiron, or assist other less-fortunate people. For this reason, I would propose to apply hourly averaging to a comprehensive tax base.

Comprehensive tax bases

Two ideal-types of comprehensive taxation have dominated the literature on tax bases: *comprehensive income* and *consumption*. Oddly, the proponents of each seem to rely on information of the other type to calculate them, as I will explain in this section.

I will refer to the traditional notion of comprehensive income taxation as *accretion*, as this is the focus of the approach. It is sometimes referred to as the Schanz-Haig-Simons definition, based upon its originators.[75] In order to calculate the income that a taxpayer has received in a given period, the idea is to compare her wealth at the beginning and end of the period, and account for her spending in that period. If all her spending has come from her wealth, then her income from the period must have been zero. However, if her spending and wealth both increased greatly, then she must have had an even larger income, equal to the addition of both. So the equation here is to add the taxpayer's net change in wealth to her spending in the period in order to calculate her taxable income for the period. Of course, the period for a lifetime-based tax calculation is a lifetime rather than a year, and so the tax would only be calculated upon the death of the taxpayer—who would have little incentive to save enough to pay the bill.

While this notion has been used—particularly in the mid-20th century—to judge real-world tax regimes, it has never been introduced. It isn't very easy to get 100% reliable consumption expenditure. It also requires the *regular valuation* of all of the wealth that individuals hold—a difficult and expensive enterprise that would leave many taxpayers discontented. It is inconvenient to government and taxpayers alike. In addition, it is not possible to accurately withhold taxation from taxpayers, meaning that all the reckoning takes place at the end of the year. This also makes the proposal less convenient, since the government and taxpayers have to wait until the end of the year before reckoning up, a time-consuming and costly process which creates uncertainty and stress.

A further worry arises to the extent that the accretion tax base mimics a feature of wealth-taxation; that people can be asked to pay tax on the value of their assets whether or not they have the liquid assets to pay their bill. This makes it harder for taxpayers to plan their affairs as they do not know for sure what their property will be worth in the future and therefore what tax they will be required to pay. It would make it more difficult for people to carry out whatever plans that they have as the value of something they own could suddenly soar. For example, someone may build their perfect home on land that later becomes very valuable—perhaps because a natural resource has been discovered or because it is located in an economically booming area. If the person decides to sell their home, then I see no problem in taxing their windfall. However, the accretion tax base would result in a large tax liability while they still desire to stay, meaning that the owners would have to sell their land to pay the bill. I do not think that it is right, therefore, to tax unrealised windfalls as the accretion tax base does.

For these and other reasons, many thinkers have proposed to calculate taxation on the basis of the value of what people *consume*.[76] There are two ways to do this. The first is the *spendings tax*.[77] The information on spending would come from retailers informing the tax authority of the amount that each customer spends in their stores. The tax authority would collate the amount that each taxpayer has spent in the relevant period and tax them accordingly. Taxes are more convenient if they are withheld, which in this case would need to be undertaken by the retailers. However, unless all citizens are to pay the same proportion of all purchases in tax it would be difficult to achieve this. One way to have a progressive spendings tax would be for every taxpayer to carry an identity card which the retailer would connect to the tax-authority database in order to indicate the tax that should be added to the purchase and passed on to the authority. The main worry about this method—other than people losing their identity card and being unable to purchase anything—is that it would make it difficult for customers to know in advance how much their shopping items will cost once tax is added.

The second, and more commonly advocated method to determine people's consumption, is to account for their comprehensive income and then deduct saved or invested funds from this amount. The difference between these two is assumed—reasonably enough—to have been consumed. This therefore requires the calculation of the taxpayer's total income, and for a reckoning to be made at the end of the period. Of course, this annual reckoning again makes the accurate withholding of tax difficult. When calculated on a lifetime basis, the consumption tax would presumably be best applied by taxing people when they receive any income, but to refund this tax whenever the individual invests the money.

Consumption taxes therefore provide people with a strong incentive to invest their money since this reduces their tax in the short term. However, while these investments may be economically useful, they would come at the expense of tax revenues rather than consumption, meaning that governments will probably raise less revenue from the fortunate to support the less fortunate in the short and medium term. Indeed, if people continue to pass on their wealth from generation to generation, the government will never receive revenue from economically fortunate individuals who will be able to benefit from their fortune. Utilising hourly averaging would mean, however, that the scions—or other beneficiaries—of the wealthy would not be able to convert their good fortune into a life of leisure. They would instead need to work in order to benefit from their good fortune, levelling the playing field somewhat between the fortunate and the less fortunate.

Hourly averaging therefore improves the consumption tax base. Nevertheless, refunding taxation on invested income is unnecessarily generous to the fortunate, since it would allow them a lot of economic power at the expense of tax revenues that could benefit the less fortunate. I therefore propose to adjust this aspect of consumption taxation in order to capture more revenue without falling foul of the disadvantages of the accretion tax base. I will explain this proposal in the remainder of this chapter.

The acquired income tax base

I refer to my preferred tax base as the *acquired income tax base*. This is because it attempts to apply taxation on the value of what resources the taxpayer has acquired and can now make use of. The acquired income tax base is, generally speaking, the second method of calculating consumption described above but without offering a tax refund for investing money. So on this definition, if you receive money, whatever its source, you have acquired resources in the shape of whatever you will go on to purchase with the money. Of course, you can choose to invest this money once you have paid the tax on it, but this does not mean you did not gain economic power upon receipt of it.

The above description indicates that when someone obtains resources of value x, this amount (x) should be added to the individual's tax calculation. However, where someone receives money and then spends it on something it is only the *initial* money income that counts as income; their new purchase would not count as income as well. This is because when the individual exchanged their money for something else they did not *gain* anything—they merely exchanged money for something of the same value as the money.[78]

This shows us that any receipt of money—physical or electronic—would count as acquired income for its recipient. However, it also implies that the receipt of *anything of money value* would also count as income—though I will discuss exemptions below. After all, if non-monetary gains were not included then everyone would simply convert money into a different form of property and then give that item of property to their intended recipient. The recipient would then convert the property back into money in order to do with it what they wish, while avoiding tax entirely. The market value of any property gained at the time of receipt should therefore be added to the gross tax reckoning of the taxpayer.

Sometimes people exchange items for one another without money changing hands, such as in barter trade. Alternatively, someone could exchange money for an item, such as purchasing something from a classified advertisement. In these cases, no income would accrue to either person. However, in some transfers like this tax *would* be due. This would apply where someone is *attempting to benefit another* by offering them something for another item that is worth less, such as if a parent offers to swap a new car for the older one owned by their daughter. In this case, the *difference* in the value of the two cars should be counted as a *gain* to—and therefore income for—the daughter. I will discuss these "partial gifts" in greater detail in the following section.

For now, I wish to make clear that it makes no difference whether the gain comes from an employer, a relative, or a friend. The *source* of the gain does not matter. It also does not matter what form the gain takes; gains to the taxpayer of any kind should be added to their gross-income tally and therefore subject to taxation. Gains can appear in the form of money, items of property, or services rendered for free or at a discount count as income. Indeed, where income is taxed so comprehensively, the authorities would have to pay extra attention to non-monetary forms of income, since these can be used by the unscrupulous in an attempt to avoid taxation. Perquisites (perks) from employers, excepting resources that are strictly necessary to undertake the work, should count as additional income for the employee. I will discuss issues of obtaining such information later in this chapter.

Gifts are included as income at their value upon receipt. An exception should be made for non-financial gifts below a certain value (for example up to the value of ten hours of work at the minimum net wage), since these are generally tokens of affection rather than forms of resource transfer. Small *financial gifts* should receive no such exemption since money cannot be given for sentimental reasons, but only as a means of resource transfer. While I have suggested that small non-financial gifts should be exempted, this should be limited in order to avoid the creation of a loophole. So, there should be a limit on the cumulative value of such gifts in any given period from any one person to another. For example, perhaps a limit of 10 tax-free gifts in a year and that the value of tax-free gifts in a year should not exceed one hundred hours of minimum wage income. Another exception could perhaps be allowed for those who receive unwanted gifts. Those who immediately sell their gifts could be allowed to count their gift at its resale value rather than its purchase value. So in the—unlikely—event that someone gives another a brand new car and the recipient immediately sells it as a second-hand car, the sale value could count rather than the amount initially spent on the car.

To be clear, there may be some benefits to individuals that should not count as income. These would include some government benefits that are provided either universally to those who meet certain criteria or on the basis of need. So if a disabled person is provided with aids in order to enable them to have capabilities similar to those of able-bodied individuals then this should not count as income. A further example is that of childhood education, which should be provided by government. Those who receive the educational provision available to all children should not have this counted as income on their tax account. I will discuss the issue of childhood and the lifetime tax in the following chapter, where I will also discuss the options for providing—and taxing—universal old-age pension income.

Determining "gains"

The examples of acquisition given above are relatively simple; they involve the transfer of money or an item of property to a person. In this section I will explain more difficult cases, all of which rely on the basic intuition of whether the individual taxpayer has newly gained some resources that they did not have previously. These complex cases are those of *partial gifts, capital gains,* and *investment returns.* These are all forms of income that should be prioritised sources of taxation, given that they are based upon windfalls or rents for the recipient.

I described in the previous section that an item of property could be sold from one person to another—the (non-profit-making) returns from which *would not* be taxable—or that an item could be gifted from one person to another—which *would* count as taxable income. However, not all exchanges will be so clear-cut. Sometimes someone may allow someone to buy something at a reduced rate as a favour—such as someone selling their unwanted furniture at a discount to a friend. In this case, the *difference* between the market value of the item and the amount paid is a gift to the recipient. The transferred item is a *partial gift* and partial exchange. Where gifts are taxable, some people may feel tempted to agree to transfer resources at less than their value in order to avoid taxation. I will discuss this possible form of income fraud in the following section.

A more familiar form of income would continue to be taxable under the acquired income tax base; *capital gain.* This is the gain people receive on items of property that are sold for more than they were initially purchased for. This gain would be included in the income of the taxpayer who profits from a sale, since the person is acquiring resources when selling their property. However, I would suggest that allowance should be made for inflation when calculating capital gains, at the same rate as that utilised in the lifetime taxation calculation as described in the following chapter.

Investment income is another type of income that would continue to be taxed according to acquired income. The problem with taxing investment income on a lifetime basis is that it is not clear whether any investment returns represent a loss on the investment or not—most investments do not have a single purchase and sale point like the items of property on which capital gains are calculated. Taxing *all* investment returns as income would discriminate against productive investments; it would make investments in property that tends to increase in value, and indeed straightforward gambling, relatively more attractive due to their lower tax. Ignoring investment returns, on the other hand, would leave a prime source of tax revenue untapped, reducing the scope for taxing the more fortunate to help the less fortunate.

In order to tax investment revenues while encouraging investment in productive enterprise, I propose that a special calculation should apply in order determine income from *registered investments*. By registered investments I mean those financial investments which are regulated and which are intended to provide incentives for investment in institutions (public and private). Examples therefore include savings accounts, bonds, and stock market investments.

This special calculation would attempt to tax returns to investments *only when the individual makes a profit on their total lifetime investments*. This requires an account with the tax authority which records the value of all of the investments that taxpayers make from their net funds at the time of purchase. Call this the *cumulative capital invested* by the taxpayer. The authorities would subtract any returns from this amount in order to calculate the *outstanding investment capital* the investor has. Any investment returns received by a taxpayer will not be taxed as long as she is a net investor with negative net outstanding investment capital recorded on her account. Another way to think about this is that the investor should be able to get her initial stake returned to her—it came out of her personal funds and so should return to those personal funds.

However, investment returns that the taxpayer receives once her returns exceed her initial investments—that is, once her outstanding investment capital is below zero—would count as taxable income. So once the investor is making a profitable return on the entirety of her lifetime investments, she will pay tax upon her returns. Of course, she can later make further investments which would put her back into the category of a net overall investor, in which case she would be eligible for tax-free investment returns again.

Imagine Pablo invests fifty pounds a year in each of twenty years, as described in table 4.1. Assume that there is no inflation or deflation during this time. Pablo receives one pound a year from each fifty pounds invested. He will dispose of the investments twenty five years after his first investment, and thereby recoup his investment of one thousand pounds. In the twenty-fifth year he will become a net beneficiary of his investments, and will have £285 of his returns added to his taxable income. His investments and records are explained in the following table. His "outstanding investment capital" records are calculated by subtracting his cumulative returns from his cumulative investments.

Table 4.2: Investment outlay, returns and taxation

Year	1	2	3	4	5	6	7	8	9	10	11	12	13
Investment	50	50	50	50	50	50	50	50	50	50	50	50	50
Cumulative capital invested	50	100	150	200	250	300	350	400	450	500	550	600	650
Gross Income: sale or returns	1	2	3	4	5	6	7	8	9	10	11	12	13
Cumulative returns	1	3	6	10	15	21	28	36	45	55	66	78	91
Outstanding invested capital	49	97	144	190	235	279	322	364	405	445	484	522	559
Taxable income	0	0	0	0	0	0	0	0	0	0	0	0	0

Year	14	15	16	17	18	19	20	21	22	23	24	25
Investment	50	50	50	50	50	50	50	0	0	0	0	0
Cumulative capital invested	700	750	800	850	900	950	1,000	1,000	1,000	1,000	1,000	1,000
Gross return	14	15	16	17	18	19	19	19	19	19	19	19
Total returns	105	120	136	153	171	190	209	228	247	266	285	1,285
Outstanding invested capital	595	630	664	697	729	760	791	772	753	734	715	-285
Taxable income	0	0	0	0	0	0	0	0	0	0	0	285

With such a system in place, no doubt many taxpayers would only pay tax on their investments upon retirement or death. This is therefore favourable to taxpayers in a similar fashion to the consumption tax base. However, the tax authority does not have to wait indefinitely for the revenue. As I will propose in the following chapter, taxpayers would pay tax on profits of their assets upon their death—known as *constructive realisation*—and so any investment gains the taxpayer makes would be taxed upon their death at the latest.

An important feature of this cumulative lifetime treatment of investment income is that it allows investors *who lose money* on one investment to *offset this* against their taxation of future investment income.[79] If each investment were treated as a separate taxable entity, then there would be no offsetting. While having no offsetting feature would increase tax revenues it would have the unfortunate side-effect that people would avoid risky investments; the gains would be heavily taxed but the loss would be lost. This means that innovative investors will be much less likely to risk resources on ventures even if they think them likely to be more profitable than other—less forward thinking—investors do. The offsetting feature of the cumulative investment recording account system would mean that an investor with several risky ventures is as likely to do well as one with several "safe" investments. Accounting for total cumulated investment therefore encourages investment in new and innovative projects which may or may not pay-off.

Calculating acquired income

Calculating the acquired income tax base I have just described requires more information than most tax authorities currently collect. In this section I will outline how I envisage it to be possible to collect this information without causing too much inconvenience to the tax authorities or taxpayers. As I indicated in the introduction, I think that technology can be utilised to improve taxation, and it should be possible to make the process as simple, fast, and accurate as possible by automatically sharing information.

The primary source of information would be from *financial organisations*. These would inform the tax authority of all transactions made into the accounts of individual taxpayers. I would also suggest that with a more comprehensive tax base in place, financial organisations could even take over the role of withholding taxation currently primarily undertaken by employers. If this were so, then by default all incoming financial resources would count as income and be taxed, with exceptions applied in approved cases of the type I will list below. In order to enable such public checking, all accounts would need to be attributed to a publicly known and verifiable person or legal entity—ruling out secretive accounts, businesses which do not name their owners, and perpetual trusts.

I mentioned that some forms of financial income would be exempted from inclusion in taxable income. One obvious exception to the inclusion of incoming financial transfers as income would be transfers an individual makes between his own accounts. In these cases he is not receiving any additional resources—merely moving his resources around. Another exception is that of not-yet profitable investments as described in the previous section. A third exemption arises where someone has received money as part of an approved expense claim from their employer or a refund from a shop. These claims would have to be approved by the tax authority in order to be exempted from inclusion as taxable income.

The fourth and final exception would be for sold items, where the money represents an exchange of an item for money. In order to accurately record these sales, I propose a further use of information technology. I suggest that there should be *asset registers* of (a) expensive types of property, and (b) those which can increase in value. There are already registers for land and vehicles—two prominent types of expensive asset that are traded—and these registers should be integrated with the tax system. Additional registers could be inaugurated for jewellery, art works, furniture, and so on. When ownership changes, the new owner would need to have their name listed on the relevant register, and both parties would be required to accept the transaction and the amount transferred. Furthermore, retailers should be required to inform the tax authorities of any significant purchase with cash—should cash still exist—with a record of the item and its purchaser.

The asset registers would be integrated with the tax authority computer system, and taxpayers could use their secure online account with the tax authority in order to confirm their transfers and the amounts paid. The amount agreed between the parties will be reliable. This is because the seller would want the price recorded to be lower in order to reduce the amount of capital gain on the item, while the purchaser would want the stated amount as high as possible as this will reduce the gain on which they would have to pay tax when they sell it. Taxpayers would only collude to lie about the price where they wish to shift a tax liability from one person to another as a form of gift and would therefore have to declare if the transfer were between people known to one another. This would trigger a greater chance of checks or further investigation by the tax authority. Failing to declare the true exchange price or the pre-existing relationship between the parties could be made a punishable offence.

All four of these exemptions could be tracked and undertaken automatically by a well-designed tax computer system. This system would be integrated with the investment system described in the previous section and the asset registers described in the previous paragraphs. The system would also be integrated with an online account for each taxpayer. This account would enable taxpayers to update their information on gifts and transfers as and when they happen. Taxpayers would be encouraged to record these details this as soon as possible, as it would greatly improve accuracy. Annual assessments could be replaced with a regular—perhaps annual—declaration, in which taxpayers would have a chance to estimate their income from small gifts and confirm that their accounts are up-to-date. Again, failing to declare acquired income at this point in time would be a punishable offence.

Obtaining information on acquired income

The calculations described in the above section would all take place automatically using the tax computer system. However, in this section I will discuss worries about information that will not be as readily forthcoming, and explain the methods by which the authorities would reduce the scope for fraud and the likelihood of getting away with fraud. As such, there is some overlap with chapter seven, which describes the methods for dealing with hour credit fraud.

One major worry with the acquired income tax base is that gift-givers will fail to declare their gifts accurately or will collude to misstate the price spent on an item of property. The two tax authority responses to this are to uncover a sufficient amount of information and to check the values on a sample of the transfers. This would be a random sample, but the tax computer system would seek out exchanges that are more likely to be inaccurate for further investigation. The system would arrange further—human—investigation of items sold between people known to one another and also those that have taken place for a value less than would be expected. The expected values would be based upon comparison with similar transfers taking place of items of a similar type, perhaps in relation to a previous valuation or its price when last exchanged. Experts in the relevant field would be called upon to check the amounts stated and anti-fraud officers would further investigate any suspicious transactions.

Indeed, the idea would be to collect as much relevant information as possible in order that the computer system can analyse metadata to flag up suspicious individuals and transactions, and that tax auditors will be armed with a lot of information. One useful piece of information will be the amount the individual spends on consumption, including information about what they purchase. If they purchase more or less than most people of one particular type of item this could indicate a legitimate focus—or lack of focus—in that particular area of spending or that they receive gifts of that type—or all other types. Indeed, there is no reason why retailers cannot be asked to automatically provide information of the type of produce that individuals and businesses purchase in order to make audits more comprehensive. So a trip to a supermarket could result in a message to the tax authority computer than the taxpayer has spent $x on perishable food, $y on non-perishable food, $z on drinks, and $w on toiletries, for example.

A further source of information would be the public itself, who would be asked to share information about neighbours or colleagues who appear to live beyond their stated means. The basic tax and income information for any named individual or for the anonymous residents of any address should be publicly available.[80] This might include their lifetime totals, plus their recent totals. Any information provided by members of the public would be added to the files of the taxpayer and could be drawn upon in an audit and any further proceedings.

As I have indicated, random as well as targeted audits would be necessary in order to confirm the veracity of the tax statements. These could include in some cases an assessment of all of the property owned by the individual performed by a team of investigators and assessors. If a taxpayer has property which would have cost more in value than their legally received income and known consumption then this alone would be proof that they have undertaken income fraud.

While these procedures do not guarantee complete accuracy, it would make it much harder for people to evade taxation. Remember also that the only thing Al Capone was ever convicted of was tax fraud. The thorough enforcement of an acquired income tax base—as well as requiring hour credits only from reputable businesses—would make illicit activities much more difficult for those engaging in criminal activity for profit. This would provide an additional route to convict criminals even if other evidence was not forthcoming. This might not stop criminal activity, but it would mean that criminals would have to put a lot more time, effort, and thought into covering their tracks.

I will now discuss a final form of income that is difficult to detect using the above means; perks for workers. Companies may opt to pay workers less but spend the money instead on providing services that benefit the workers. This is likely to increase where highly-paid workers are taxed at a much higher rate, as they would be according to the highly progressive tax rates described in chapter one. The main means to uncover such activity would be during audits on employers. While I would argue that corporation tax should be removed if the proposals set out in this book were introduced internationally, it would still be necessary to perform thorough audits on companies and charities in order to ensure that they are fulfilling their stated function and are not a front for illicit activities. One purpose of these audits is to ensure that money spent by employers are directed towards the purpose of the enterprise and not utilised as a means to evade income taxation.

Again, with regard to companies, the tax authority could receive information from various sources that would lead them to investigate further. This would include information from members of the public and whistle-blowers from within institutions, as well as unusual spending by staff members. This information could be noted on the file of the employer, building up a picture which may lead later auditors to further investigate and prosecute company owners and employers. Institutions which have several indicators of suspicion could be subject to further secret investigations—such as investigators posing as customers and attempting to purchase products in order to check the official claims of the institution.

The rules on what counts as a perk would need to be clear and publicly known, but flexible over time. As Boris Bittker argued, there is nothing in the ideal of comprehensive income that tells us which perks should count as income.[81] A list would therefore have to be drawn up, for example that there should be a limit on the tax-free compensation available for certain kinds of expense, such as hotel stays and meals while on business trips. The authorities would need to monitor job applications and negotiations in order to ensure that any legal perks are not being increasingly utilised as an alternative form of payment. They would therefore need to have the ability to change the rules accordingly—albeit with suitable public consultation and democratic oversight, as well notice ahead of the change.

I have indicated some of the means that the authorities would have to uncover the information required to check the declarations taxpayers make regarding their acquired income. I will discuss fraud further when discussing hour credit fraud in chapter seven and it should be clear that there would be overlap in the means to uncovering hour credit fraud and income fraud. However I have taken the opportunity to indicate some of the means to avoiding income fraud alongside the explanation of the acquired income tax base.

Conclusion

I have shown that hourly averaging is compatible with several tax bases. It could be applied to wage income alone, but this would fail to integrate the amount of several kinds of fortune that taxpayers have (and which would ideally be taken account of). Comprehensive taxation—with hourly averaging—would more accurately tax individuals in accordance with their level of fortune. However, the traditional accretion conception of income is unattractive for several reasons.

The consumption tax ideal is more attractive than labour or accretion taxation, and even more so when combined with hourly averaging. However, I proposed a hybrid proposal that retains some elements of the comprehensive income ideal. I referred to this as the acquired income tax base, as it taxes people on the value of the resources that they acquire in accordance with their value upon acquisition. This represents the pre-tax purchasing power that the individual obtains over their lifetime, and therefore combines the attractive features of the accretion and consumption tax base proposals.

CHAPTER FIVE

LIFETIME AVERAGING

IN SHAKESPEARE'S *As You Like It*, Jaques famously described a person's life as consisting of "seven ages," and while I will not follow these particular stages there is a certain parallel in the way I approach this chapter. This is because I will split the discussion into several chronological stages in the life of a taxpayer in order to present further requirements and considerations that arise when moving from annual to lifetime taxation.

The seven stages—or events—that I discuss are those of birth, childhood (until the age of majority), adulthood, marriage, divorce, retirement, and death. These allow me to discuss the various issues that arise with regard to lifetime averaging and the utilisation of the acquired income tax base. Many of the issues discussed would arise with other tax bases, though I will present rules tailored for an acquired income tax base.

I will begin with birth, since this is no doubt a sensible time to set up someone's fledgling lifetime tax account. However, I should note that immigrants would have their local tax account set up at the announcement of their arrival. I will discuss the treatment of international citizens in chapter eight. The issues arising from setting up taxation accounts also links to the transition from an annual to a lifetime calculation and from a broad tax base to an acquired income base. I will discuss the issues of transition specifically in chapter eight.

Along with the setting up of tax accounts I will explain how they will be brought into full effect for those who reach adulthood. When discussing the progress of taxation through adulthood I will take the opportunity to discuss an issue of particular importance when undertaking lifetime income calculations; inflation. Another set of changes that can occur during adulthood is that people can join their lives together, and that this conjoining can come to an end. I therefore explain that where people combine their economic lives they can also combine their tax accounts. A further change happens when people retire from work, and I present the various options for the treatment of retirees under a lifetime hourly averaging tax system with an acquired income tax base. The final section presents the process of closing an account upon the death of the taxpayer and how this links to the disbursement of the estate of the deceased.

Beginnings

If hourly averaging will only be applied upon income from work then an individual's tax account need only begin when they first obtain hour credits—for example when they start working. The tax authority, of course, would do well to set one up in advance of the maturation of children in order to enable the individual's taxation calculation to start without any difficulties. However, if lifetime taxation is applied on a comprehensive tax base, such as that of *acquired income* which I explained in the previous chapter, then it is necessary to begin an individual's tax account at birth and to apply it during their childhood. I should note that, in addition, any immigrant would also need to have their personal tax account set up upon arrival in the state.

Children obviously receive many resources during their childhood from their guardians, and sometimes from others such as Grandparents. Where there is a lifetime tax account on comprehensive income I would propose to include childhood income in the tax base. However, children should not be attributed as having had income for the items that are considered necessary for the life of a dependent child. As a result, most children would not have any income attributed to them when they reach adulthood.

However, some children should have received gross and net income attributed to their account, just as is done when an adult receives a gift. This is necessary to avoid the creation of a "childhood gift" loophole. If gifts to children were not counted as income then it would be possible for people to make their gifts to their loved ones without incurring any tax by transferring it before the child becomes an adult. Of course, people should be able to give gifts to children and the majority of these should not count as taxable. However, where these gifts are of great expense then they are not simply gifts to enhance a childhood but are instead done with the purpose of avoiding taxation, then they should count as taxable income for that child. After all, children generally do not understand the money value of gifts and are usually satisfied with relatively cheap forms of entertainment.

I would therefore suggest that any gifts above a certain value, for example of the value of 100 hour credits at the minimum net income level, should be counted as income on their tax-free account. There should also be a cumulative limit on the gifts that children should be able to receive in a year from all sources. This could be set at something like the value of 500 hour credits. Since children cannot have received any hour credits any gifts that they receive above this value would be immediately taxed. There are then two options. One option is to force the sale of the gift—if it is not money anyway—and apply the money to the gross income received on the child's emerging tax account. If the sale is forced then the child has not received the gift and they will not have any net income counted on their account, only gross income. This gross money will later enhance the income available to the child. After all, the income would be on their tax account for the remainder of their life and when they become an adult and obtain hour credits it will enhance their net hourly average.

In the case of some gifts, of course, it is not possible or necessary to enforce the sale of the item. There may be cases in which a child receives a non-financial gift that is slightly over the value of the limit. In these cases the child should be able to keep the gift, but the *additional amount* should be applied to her tax account as gross *and* net income. Financial gifts can of course be readily split into taxable and non-taxable portions.

It is not possible to tax valuable gifts if they do not take the form which would allow them to be resold. An example of such a gift would be a holiday. Taking a child on a holiday is a commendable thing. However, it would not be advisable to allow benefactors to provide extremely expensive holidays as a means to provide gifts for individuals without it counting as income. As a result, it would be necessary to specify a maximum amount which can be spent on a child in a given year. Children who have a holiday of great expense provided for them should have any spending above this amount applied as net and gross income on their tax account.[82]

Lifetime taxation opens up a further policy possibility regarding the treatment of education. Some children obtain a superior education due to the resources spent upon them. This is often intended to give children a positional benefit over the other children of their age-group. The lifetime tax accounting would make it possible to provide a counter-incentive to those who would spend resources on their children in this way.[83] This could be done by counting the money spent on a child's education above the value of that provided by the state to all children as a form of income to that individual. This again would be counted as gross and net income on their tax account and would result in an increased rate of taxation for their adult lives to compensate others for their relative disadvantage. In practice, this policy would likely cause a substantial reduction in the additional resources spent on childhood education in order to provide positional advantages for children.

Reaching majority

I have said that it would be necessary for the tax authority to set up a tax account for individuals prior to adulthood, and at birth where the tax base is a comprehensive one. In this section I will consider issues surrounding the move to a fully-operational tax account. This process will of course mirror that which would be applied in the transition from an annual system to a full lifetime system, which I will discuss in chapter eight.

Once our individual reaches adulthood, which could be set at 16, 17, or 18, she will be able to work and obtain hour credits. I would suggest that if education is not compulsory beyond the age of 16 then hour credits should be available from this point. However, it may be sensible to apply additional rules on young adults, for example a requirement to undertake a certain amount of education or training. Another rule might be to limit the number of hour credits that young adults can obtain in a week during this period, perhaps at the same rate as those who receive additional hour credits. This would put further education on the same foothold as low-paid work for those in the transitional phase from childhood to adulthood, which may otherwise incentivise young adults to make decisions that are not in their interests or those of society.

A complication arises, however, since some children work for money. This would have to be treated differently than adult work. Some children do low-paid part-time work—such as a paper round—when they are younger than 16. These jobs can probably be ignored for the purpose of taxable income and hour credits as long as the jobs are restricted—as they should be—to low hours (and therefore low incomes). A minority of children may have more highly paid work as actors or singers, which is a more complicated issue. I would suggest that the majority of the income from such activities, perhaps after allowing a certain tax-free stipend, should be taxed as gross income on the tax account of the individual in question. While this means that child actors would not receive the income from their work, they would obtain higher income during their adult lives as a result of their activities.

When people's tax accounts fully begin—so this point also applies to immigrants—it is necessary to ensure that the correct amount of childhood net and gross income have been recorded. In order to undertake investigations and audits on the individual during her adult life, it is also necessary to have the information on the property that they own at the point at which citizens move into adulthood. Therefore young adults will be asked to itemise what they own.[84] This property can be valued, and if it is above a specified value—indicating that they are much better-off than the average young adult—then it may be advisable to count some of this additional wealth as taxable income.[85] Perhaps the young adult could be offered the choice between selling some of their items in order to pay their tax bill, or alternatively to keep their property and begin their account with a debt to the tax authority.

Adulthood and inflation

The tax treatment of adults is relatively straightforward for the most part. People's tax accounts would continue in ways that I have described since chapter one. Taxpayers would live their lives, accumulating gross income and hour credits, and receiving their appointed net income as they go. They can do what they want with their resources as long as they follow the laws of their society and provide the tax authority with the information that they are required to. However, I will take the opportunity of this section to describe one issue that does arise with taxation over a longer timeframe than a year, that of *inflation*.

Annual taxation is usually untroubled by inflation since prices do not change very much within a year.[86] However, over many years prices can change by a large amount. If the tax rates were set upon inauguration of the system, the prices to which they refer will be worth substantially less thirty or a hundred years later. For example, a high wage in 1910 would be a very low wage in 2010. Cumulative systems could deal with this by accounting for inflation when creating the many tax tables for those of different ages. However, this would not be fair. There are several different ways of dealing with inflation and I will present one that solves the issue at hand. This is to rewrite past figures in line with inflation.

The idea behind this approach is to account for past income and taxation at *current price levels*, which can be easily achieved by indexing. The tax-rate graph therefore also has to change each year in line with inflation, just as governments currently adjust the tax-rates of annual taxes. This means that the tax graph will retain its shape but shift along the gross income axis in line with inflation or deflation every year. This is a very straightforward process with a modern computerised system. Thus, indexing past income is perfectly fair because the tax-rate will have been altered as well. To summarise; *both the tax rates and the historical payments of all taxpayers should be indexed to inflation*.

One downside of this indexing, compared to annual tax calculations, is that it is more difficult for individuals to make simple calculations about their future income and tax liability. The inconvenience is minor as individuals will be able to make accurate estimates—inflation would hopefully be low. Furthermore, individuals will have to make assumptions about all the other variables anyway, since no one knows exactly what will happen in the future. As calculations about future earnings are never entirely exact, they can only ever serve as a guide anyway. This minor inconvenience is a triviality when compared against the aim of having a fair tax system.

A second concern regarding revaluing in line with inflation is that it will create a threshold point, which will mean that investors may have artificial incentives to make trades before or after the revaluation in order to reduce the capital gain or tax-rate on an investment. In response to this, I would point out that in most years the inflation rate should be low and so the incentives would be limited. Secondly, if this was felt to be an issue then it would be perfectly possible to revalue all values in line with inflation every six months rather than every year. Since the lifetime hourly averaging tax system is an on-going one there is no reason not to do this if the advantages outweigh the costs of adding a further calculation.

Merging and demerging accounts

I have said that the tax accounts of adults are relatively straightforward. However, a potential complication arises where individuals join together to form a single family unit, combining their incomes and liabilities. In this case, it would appear inappropriate to apply separate tax calculations upon them. However, to close old accounts and begin a new joint account would not be fair to those who have received unearned income.[87] This is because closing someone's account would bar them from the advantage of such gross income on their future net income when they receive further hour credits. Fortunately, it should be possible to *merge* lifetime tax accounts together from a specified date, keeping past figures from both accounts.

Couples would need to inform the authorities of the date at which they will officially combine all of their wealth, from which they will share their income and liabilities. The authorities will prepare a new combined account which would automatically redirect any subsequent income from each of the previous accounts into the combined account. The old accounts will therefore lie dormant and the combined account will be used for all tax calculations. The same tax-rate graph can of course apply, since there are now two people who can obtain hour credits just as there are now two people who can obtain an income.

It would be necessary for the authorities to obtain full information of the wealth that each individual takes into their newly combined economic lives. This would be necessary in case there is a later divorce settlement and account demerger. Such a demerger is perfectly possible as the previous individual accounts would be reinstated. The hour credits and gross income received during the combined period would be split in half and added to each re-instated account. I imagine that divorce procedures would be much simpler with this system than the present one. This is because the lifetime tax system and wealth assessments at the start and end of the merged account would provide much more information on the parties.

There may be a windfall or tax cost to mergers and demergers since the combined account may have a different lifetime tax liability than the previous account or accounts had. This could occur because the tax-rate might be different for the combined account, though the difference should not be too great. The authorities could allow taxpayers to pay-off such debts over a long period in order not to discourage people from merging or demerging accounts in accordance with their economic circumstances. They might also spread windfalls over a long period in order to ensure that people do not undertake such mergers simply to obtain a windfall. The authorities should probably also monitor the true living arrangements of those who obtain large windfalls from account mergers or demergers, to deter those tempted to form sham marriages for taxation purposes.[88]

Retirement and pensions

Another area which raises questions for lifetime taxation is how best to deal with retirement and pensions. Taxing retirees is a difficult issue for the same reason that retirement is a complicated financial issue for retirees: no one knows how long they will live for. For this reason people purchase annuities that promise to pay out a set amount of money to people at a regular interval for the remainder of their life and governments provide the elderly with a universal pension. There are several possible options with regard to retirement and pensions, and on this topic I will present more than one. I do this because while it is important to avoid the wrong combination of options, there are at least two sensible approaches available and it would be necessary to undertake further research and thought before choosing between them. In this section I will discuss some sensible options regarding the inclusion of such pension and annuity payments with hourly lifetime taxation.

In some respects, retirement is a much less problematic issue for hourly averaging than it is for time-passed averaging. Time-passed averaging would enable those who live a long life to receive large rebates on their previous tax payments. The downside of this is that it would reduce the power of governments to control and anticipate their tax revenues and liabilities.[89] Nevertheless, it would be possible to mimic this tax-rebate approach with hourly averaging by providing hour credits for the retired. These hour credits would reduce the tax-rate that retirees would face on their lifetime gross income and would thereby cause a rebate. This is certainly one option as a way of providing a pension to retired workers, and it would be administratively inexpensive. If hour credits are provided for those over a specified age then it could be combined with a *gross* income payment made to all retirees. This payment would help to keep the tax-rate of the retiree at a level that corresponds more closely to their relative fortune during their lives.

Instead of providing retirees with hour credits, it would be possible simply to stop people from receiving hour credits beyond a set age, perhaps allowing an exception for those who continue to perform work for money beyond this point. If retirees were not provided with hour credits then it would be necessary to provide them with tax-free sources of income such as the universal old-age pension and approved annuity income. If these forms of income were not exempted from tax then the retiree would face an ever increasing tax-rate over time which would mean that most of their further income would be lost to taxation.

However, while I would tend to prefer the latter, tax-free income approach over the free hour credit alternative, I will offer one note of caution. If annuities are allowed to be received as tax-free income there should be strict limits on these annuities. Strict limits are necessary in order to avoid the creation of a loophole whereby fortunate individuals can reduce their lifetime taxation by funnelling resources into a tax-free annuity. I will therefore present the following retirement plan, which I think should be the only source of tax-free income for retirees over and above that of the universal pension.

Governments often provide people of working age with incentives to save for their retirement. This can be done for paternalist reasons, given that people are considered to be myopic when it comes to saving. It is also in the government's interest to encourage saving since it creates investment revenues for the economy and reduces the potential burden of impoverished elderly people in future decades. The UK, for example, provides a pension saving system with two main advantages for savers. The first advantage is that gains on pension investments are taxed in a much more favourable manner than other investment gains. Second, pension investors can place their *gross* income into their pension fund and thereby reduce their taxable income when they earn it. Both these policies are favourable to more economically fortunate individuals who pay a higher rate of tax, and these pension incentives are therefore a regressive policy that violates the ideal of transferring resources intended for the economically fortunate towards the less fortunate. Nevertheless, there remain strong reasons to want people to save for their retirement, and so I propose an alternative approach that retains some of these features.

The proposal I make is that it should be mandatory for a portion of each person's *net* hourly income to be placed into a pension account from which they can draw upon retirement. Pension companies could offer packages and savers would select how much of their investment should go with which package. Those who fail to select one of the providers would have their investment placed with a basic government scheme. Investment policies would all have to meet strict requirements and involve relatively safe forms of investment in order to qualify. Since the saving would correspond to the hourly average of the taxpayer, those who work a greater number of hours would have a greater amount saved in their account.

When reaching retirement age the taxpayers would be able to purchase an annuity with their mandatory pension funds, and as I have indicated this income would not be taxed. The pension would generally only be available to those over a specified age— say 60 or 65—but there should be an exemption available. This exemption would apply to those of a lower age who have a terminal illness or a relatively low life expectancy, who should be able to access their retirement savings if they wish.

People would of course be able to purchase further annuities should they choose to do so, though these annuities would be taxed. One way to do this would be to include the annuity payments as gross lifetime income and utilising the individual's lifetime tax account. As an alternative, it would be possible to have a separate progressive annual tax system applied to these additional pension funds only.

Death

I have explained that it should be possible to perform real-time tax calculations by treating each calculation as if it would be the last for the taxpayer. This was not strictly true, for reasons I will explain in this section. Unlike the ending of a tax account due to merger or demerger, the ending of a tax account as a result of death would bring about the need for the *constructive realization* of the assets held by the deceased. Not all taxpayer deaths would result in this constructive realization, of course, as in some cases the deceased will be survived by the other party to a merged account. In this case, the merged account would revert to the single account of the surviving member. Upon the death of its corresponding citizen, each tax account will have a truly final reckoning, and this will coincide with the disbursement of the taxpayer's estate.

When discussing the tax base in the previous chapter I explained the advantages of the acquired income tax-base over comprehensive income and consumption taxation. Its advantage over consumption taxation is that it does not enable resources to be transferred from generation to generation without any taxation. Its advantage over comprehensive income is that it would not require the valuation and taxation of gains until they are realised, while still requiring that all assets should be realised upon the death of the taxpayer. This is achieved by enforcing realization of the gains on assets for the purpose of taxation only upon the death of a taxpayer. Realization is also much more convenient for governments and taxpayers, since the deceased will not be party to the valuation of her assets, and the government has access to the information on the total estate of the deceased. This information is available as it is required as part of the process of bequeathing the estate of the deceased.

The process of constructively realizing the estate of the recently deceased could take a number of forms. One option would be to liquidate the estate and to transfer the money left after taxation in accordance with the wishes of the deceased or the laws regarding those who die intestate (without a will). This could be achieved by sending the entire estate to auction. However, people may often wish to bequeath *certain* items to *certain* loved ones, and it would be better not to enforce the liquidation of the estate if this is not going to be necessary in order to pay the tax bill.

There should therefore be a presumption that the heirs should be able to receive the items of property specified in a will. It is necessary, of course, to value all assets in order both to assess whether there is a taxable gain on the items and to know how much income to apply to the tax account of the recipients. The heirs should be given priority in the process, such that named items can be transferred if a) the taxes have been paid on the estate of the deceased and b) the recipient can cover the taxation due on their receipt of the item. In some cases the recipient may need to secure a loan or mortgage in order to cover the taxation and obtain the bequeathed item, and a certain amount of weeks would need to be allowed for them to find the resources to pay the tax debt that would arise.

Conclusion

In this chapter I have explained how to apply hourly averaging over the life of an individual. In doing so, I have clarified some aspects of the practicalities of hourly averaging and the application of the acquired income tax-base on a lifetime basis. I began by explaining the two beginning points of the individual's tax account. The first is when the account is set up but contains no hour credits, which could feasibly occur at the birth of the taxpayer. The account begins in full when the taxpayer reaches adulthood, at which point he can receive hour credits. Before this point children should be able to obtain resources tax-free, but if these exceed a certain limit then they should be added to the fledgling tax account, either as gross and net income or—if withheld from the child—simply as gross income.

Tax accounts are generally quite straightforward from this point on, though I have clarified three further issues in this chapter. The first issue is the method of dealing with inflation in a lifetime tax system. I argued that the regular revaluing of past tax and income figures would keep all figures in roughly the same denomination without any serious downsides. The second issue is the treatment of those who have combined all their economic affairs, for example due to marriage. This should be readily possible with hourly averaging by allowing the creation of an additional merged account for the duration of the relationship. Upon separation or the death of one of the parties the merged account would cease to exist and the hour credits and income would be split into the surviving accounts. The third issue is the tax treatment of retirement income. On this subject I described two broad alternatives. The first approach is to continue to provide retirees with hour credits, which would provide them with a retirement income. The second approach, which I prefer, is to enable retirees to have some tax-free income from appropriately appointed sources which are reasonably universal. Other retirement annuity income could be taxed on a traditional annual basis or could be included as gross lifetime income.

In the final section I explained how the lifetime tax calculation would end upon the death of the taxpayer, at which point a final reckoning of her gains would be undertaken. Once the tax on these gains has been paid from her estate, the remainder of the estate can be bequeathed in accordance with her wishes.

PART III

CHAPTER SIX

CONSTITUTIONAL REQUIREMENTS

IN THE THIRD and final part of this book I will consider, and respond to, some of the worries that people may have after reading parts one and two of the book. Essentially, I will anticipate some of the legitimate concerns that I imagine critics will have. In this chapter I will consider the constitutional rules that would need to be applied in order to placate worries about the economic effects of the proposals and the potentially troubling power relationships it may engender. In chapter seven I will consider the issue of hour credit fraud and explain how the tax authority could reduce the scope for this. In chapter eight I will discuss the issue of transitioning to an hourly tax system and the international regimes that would be compatible with hourly averaging.

In this chapter I will present two broad worries for the CLIPH-rate tax and explain the constitutional rules required in order to deal with them. The first worry is that progressive taxation and the acquired income tax-base would result in overconsumption and short-termism, which would lead to economic ruin. I explain that it would be necessary to set up a sovereign wealth fund in order to ensure continuing investment.

The bulk of this chapter explains what constitutional rules would be necessary to deal with various worries concerning power relations under the CLIPH-rate tax. The combination of lifetime averaging, the need that people would have for hour credits, and the acquired income tax base render citizens vulnerable to unscrupulous governments and government agents. I will explain several worries about power relations and what rules should be put in place to respond to them. The first worry is that the government will have too much economic power and will therefore take too much in taxation. The response to this concern is to make it difficult for governments to increase taxes by requiring a supermajority of votes in support. A second worry is that government agencies (or their agents) would have too much power compared to individuals. The response to this is to ensure judicial oversight of intelligence agents. The third and final worry concerning power imbalances arises as individuals require hour credits, meaning that those who *confer* hour credits may be in a position to manipulate or abuse them. The response to this is to ensure that it is possible to bring complaints against those who abuse their position, with the threat that serial abusers would lose their right to confer hour credits.

Would the CLIPH-rate tax cause macroeconomic damage?

The first worry I will anticipate is that the proposals I have set out would have deleterious macroeconomic consequences. I will distinguish two worries under this heading. One worry is that the system would cause overconsumption in the short term which would lead to economic decline. I will explain this below and in the following section I will describe the constitution of the Sovereign Wealth Fund which would deal with the problem. First of all, however, I will briefly deal with another worry, which is that the tax system will be too cumbersome to enable an activist monetary policy to counteract the tendency within capitalism towards economic boom and bust.

As I will explain later in this chapter, it should be made very difficult to change the tax-rates once the system is set up. This may lead some to worry that the financial ministry (known as the treasury in the UK) would not be able to enact macroeconomic policies. By macroeconomic policies, I refer to policies that are designed to stimulate the economy during times of recession and depression, and to cool the economy down during booms.[90] I have two responses to this. The first is that most other levers would still be available to governments and central banks, such as changing central bank interest rates, obtaining loans, or—in extreme situations—printing money. In addition, I would emphasise that the hourly averaging proposal would, in fact, have an automatic stabilising effect. In good times tax revenues will rise as more people pay more in tax as gross incomes and gains would increase. In bad times taxpayers would receive additional support as their tax-rates would drop if their hourly incomes dropped. The state would then act to prop-up the income of taxpayers in the short term, thus reducing the effect of any recession.

Astute commentators may worry that while these effects may stabilise the economy in the short-term, it might lead to disaster in the longer term. This relates to the second macroeconomic worry; that hourly averaging would lead to overconsumption and short-termism with terrible economic consequences. This is that the government will obtain significant revenues from taxation, and that government spending on workers or income subsidies via the hourly averaging system will drive short-term consumption at the expense of longer term investment.

At present a small number of wealthy individuals own the vast majority of the productive capacity of the economy.[91] If the CLIPH-rate tax were in place when these individuals die then the majority of these investments would be obtained by the tax authorities. This would happen because if they pass the investments on to their heirs, these beneficiaries would face a very high tax-rate and would receive a small fraction of the windfall. The rest would go into the government treasury.[92] The worry about overconsumption arises as the wealth captured in taxation would either be spent by government or would be transferred to poorer individuals via the tax system, and these poorer individuals would spend the resources rather than save them. This process would result in a loss of long-term productive capacity in favour of short term consumption, which would have significant economic effects.

As a result of the likely effects of the CLIPH-rate tax on the wealth of citizens the state would need to have a different attitude to investment than it otherwise might.[93] The tax windfalls obtained by the state during the early years of the system would need to be re-invested by the state in order to maintain the investment in the economy. Some states have already set up institutions that undertake this function, and these are usually referred to as *Sovereign Wealth Funds* (SWF for short). Alongside the CLIPH-rate tax, it would be advisable for states to integrate a SWF with the tax system in order that it could absorb the windfall tax receipts and re-invest them. The SWF would have to be very strictly regulated, though kept reasonably separate from government.

The Constitution of a Sovereign Wealth Fund

The internal structure of the SWF and its relationship to other bodies would have to be set at a constitutional level upon the introduction of hourly averaging. The SWF would be a state institution run at arms-length from the democratically elected government. It would have a brief to make safe investments and aim to generate returns (profits) wherever possible. These returns would increase the value of the fund. The fund would be staffed by those with investment and technical expertise, under the supervision of a diverse board of individuals the majority of whom would be independent from the government. These constitutional rules would be in place to ensure that governments would not use the fund to achieve short-term populist aims at the expense of the success of the fund.

The relationship between the government, the SWF, and the tax authority would be a hugely important constitutional issue, and I will discuss this now. I have said that the government should be reasonably independent from the SWF and I would suggest that this should also apply with regard to the tax authority and decisions about whether tax revenues are diverted to the government or to the SWF. I would suggest that the government should be provided with a set amount of income, which would rise automatically each year in accordance with the rate of inflation. This settlement could be initially calculated based upon the level of government spending prior to the introduction of the system. This financial settlement would, of course, exclude those activities that would be subsumed into the hourly calculation, given that many benefit payments would be taken on by the more holistic and universal tax system.

The constitutional rules could, for example, insist that the government of the day should only be able to obtain a few per cent of any tax revenues in excess of the agreed settlement amount if they were to overspend. Governments would generally have to live beyond the means of their settlement, excepting other forms of revenue—such as sin taxes and other fees and charges—that it could obtain. If the government should—due to unforeseen circumstances—find itself unable to avoid spending within its means, then it would be necessary to decide whether to draw on the SWF to make up the difference, whether to fund the deficit through borrowing, or whether to limit the revenues of the government. It would be important to ensure that the government of the day would not be able to raid the SWF, and so there should be pre-agreed formula of borrowing, spending cuts, and SWF drawdown in cases where revenues fall short. However, it should be possible to override this formula if there is sufficient agreement between the government, the opposition, the relevant monetary authorities (such as the central bank and SWF) and experts representing future generations who would be affected by the decisions.

It should be possible to change the government revenue settlement and debt-funding formula, of course. However, it should be difficult for any single actor, such as the government ministers of the day, to change these rules. There should therefore be a supermajority requirement for the democratic chamber, or perhaps agreement which includes the SWF board members and representatives of future generations. I have indicated the issues and explained the importance of strong constitutional rules over these matters. However, there has been no need to specify the exact levels of the settlements and formulas involved; I am only indicating the importance of ensuring that the relevant checks and balances are introduced at the constitutional level of the state and the institutions in question.

Abuse of power and government as Leviathan

The second set of concerns that I will respond to in this chapter fall under the heading of abuse of power. This is because in all cases the worry is that the government or its officials would wield power over individuals in ways that would make individuals either worse-off than they might otherwise be, or even leave individuals in a disastrously vulnerable position. The first such worry I will discuss is that of the government becoming a "Leviathan" which takes more tax revenue than it should, simply because it can.

The government leviathan worry has been most famously expressed in the book *The Power to Tax* by Brennan and Buchanan.[94] These authors assume that political parties will seek to obtain power by offering certain groups in society the chance of government jobs in exchange for voting for them. In order to pay for these jobs, the government will maximise tax revenues, thus taxing individuals more than they should. I think that the authors overstate the assumption regarding the innate tendency for governments to create an overtaxing Leviathan. They also place too much emphasis on economic efficiency as compared to other goals of government, such as creating a just society which should take precedence over economic efficiency. Nevertheless, the worry does arise that the government would have even more power to raise tax revenues with the CLIPH-rate tax than it does with the current annual and loophole-ridden tax system. The system fits neatly to the model of the Leviathan state imagined by Brennan and Buchanan.

The response to this concern has already been somewhat anticipated in the previous section. There should be a SWF which would absorb windfall tax revenues, thus leaving less revenue available to governments. Nevertheless, there may be a worry that governments would shift the tax-rate graph such that more revenue goes to governments and less goes to individuals. Like Brennan and Buchanan, I suggest that there should be constitutional rules to reduce the scope for over-taxation. However, unlike those authors I do not think it is necessary to undermine the tax base and encourage interna-tional tax competition (something I discuss in chapter eight) in order to respond to this problem.

I propose that government ministers should not have direct control over hourly average tax-rates. I have indicated that the rate should change in line with inflation at each period, at the same time as past values are re-valued in line with inflation. Changing the tax-rate with the CLIPH-rate tax would be an immensely more serious matter than it is with any current kind of tax. If the tax were made more generous to taxpay-ers (shifting the line on the tax-rate graph to the right), then it would trigger a large payment from government (or the SWF) to individuals. Alternatively, if the tax on individuals were increased (shifting the graph to the left), then individuals would immediately find themselves in debt to the government. Those who have lived longer under the system would face a much greater tax rebate or bill in these circumstances, due to their much greater number of hour credits.

Due to these extreme effects, it would be better not to change the tax-rate graph if at all possible. However, given that economic circumstances may change, it must be possible to do this. My suggestion would be that the most sensible approach to making tax-rate changes would be to simply alter the tax-rate at a different rate to the specified inflation-rate when the re-valuations take place. For example, the tax-rate graph could be re-valued by 2.01% when past values are changed by 2%. In this way, the government could gradually change the tax-rate of individuals over a number of years in order to correct for over-optimism or pessimism at an earlier date.

That explains the least intrusive manner to change the tax-rate when it would need to be done. I will now explain who should make this decision. The finance minister (known as the "Chancellor of the Exchequer" in the UK) should have the power to provide a slightly more favourable tax-rate for individuals than the prevailing inflation rate. However, there should be constitutional barriers on the ability of the government to increase—or more rapidly decrease—the tax on individuals. The government would need to obtain additional support for such a change. This might be the requirement for a supermajority in the main democratic chamber, the agreement of the SWF board, and the agreement of representatives of future generations. Perhaps it could require the agreement of an extraordinary board meeting containing members from these democratic and constitutional institutions.

It may be considered wise to go beyond these measures in order to ensure that governments are not profligate with their spending. Additional restrictions could be placed on the quantity of borrowing that governments may undertake, for example. The same supermajority requirements could be imposed on governments seeking to exceed a certain amount of borrowing—either by an absolute amount or as a proportion of previous borrowing—in a particular period. I am less convinced of the need to introduce restrictions of this kind on governments, particularly as it could give too much power to an unreasonable opposition party who could attempt to hold the government to ransom when it needs to increase borrowing.

Limits on government agencies

A second type of fear regarding government power is that government agencies and their agents would have too much power to interfere in people's lives. Government agents such as the police and intelligence services currently have the scope to utilise a reasonable amount of power over individuals. Twentieth century technological advances rendered oppressive totalitarian states possible, though fortunately western democratic states have shown that it is possible to allow individuals to have a reasonable degree of freedom through the use of the legal process and the rule of law. Nevertheless, the CLIPH-rate tax would provide governments with additional information about every individual, as well as the power to make life impossible for individuals by interfering with their tax account. For example, the government could block the receipt of hour credits for those who it deems undesirable or overly critical. The worry is that government agencies or their agents could utilise this additional power in unacceptable ways.

The two best guards against the abuse of power by government agencies are a strong legal culture of rights, and the constant vigilance of the population over their government in case it should seek to remove or undermine these legal protections. A society with the CLIPH-rate tax would be much more equal, and it would be very difficult for power-hungry individuals to get to positions where they would have access to great political power and financial power at the same time.

Furthermore, we can hope that citizens of a more equal society would monitor their politicians and their actions more effectively. It is conceivable that these features of the society would mean there would be less scope—and incentive—for unscrupulous people to take hold of the mechanisms of the state.

Governments should not be interfering in the lives of their citizens, and so there should be no possibility for governments or their agents to interfere with the tax accounts that individuals have. As such, the tax authority anti-fraud agency—I discussed fraud in chapter four and will discuss it further in the following chapter—should be entirely separate from the agencies involved in other forms of security. These agencies should not routinely share information, though it will of course be necessary for them to obtain information from one another in the course of their investigations. Nevertheless, there should be restrictions on the channels through which the agencies could obtain information. The tax fraud agencies should work closely with the security agencies on investigations into individuals and gangs of individuals suspected of large-scale fraud and other criminal enterprise. However, the security agencies should require judicial agreement before obtaining any information about the real-time financial activities and whereabouts of an individual. The judge or magistrate would need to be convinced that the provision of such information was necessary as part of a legitimate and appropriate investigation.

The checks and balances indicated above would make it more difficult for rogue government agencies and agents to utilise tax information in an improper or undemocratic manner. It would also mean that governments which intend to act in an authoritarian manner would have to go against the constitution or make it publicly known that they intend to change the rules. If a government did undertake to make such a change,then it would be up to right thinking citizens to stand against it, alongside the judiciary.

The power of those who confer hour credits

The final worry on the subject of power relations refers to the power of those who confer hour credits over those who need hour credits. In order to have any income citizens need to obtain hour credits, and this means that they depend upon receiving them from someone with the right to confer them. I will discuss the rules regarding the conferring of hour credits in the following chapter on hour credit fraud. Nevertheless, it is possible to indicate in this section how to abate the concern that those who confer hour credits will be able to exploit or abuse those who depend upon the hour credits they control.

The first point in response to this concern is that employers should have complaint procedures against managers, such that any one manager would not wield too much power over any employee. However, this may not be sufficient in all companies, as several managers could collude in exploitation and abuse. Furthermore, some companies might be so small that there is only one person—the owner—who has the right to confer the hour credits. In these cases, workers should be able to take legal action against managers who abuse their position. Employees are unlikely to find themselves entirely at the economic mercy of an employer under a system of hourly averaging. The first reason is because employees can always leave their job and obtain hour credits from the guaranteed work programme. Second, the reduction in minimum wage for employers and generous subsidies for very low-paid workers should mean that there would not be the levels of unemployment currently experienced. An abused employee would have the option to leave their job with less of a penalty than they would face under the current tax and benefit system.

I have said that employees can always fall back on the guaranteed work scheme. However, this means that abuse or exploitation by those who confer hour credits as part of this scheme is *more of a worry* than exploitation by other employers.

Those in the guaranteed work scheme do not have the alternatives and so those who seek to abuse and exploit others may be attracted to a job as a guaranteed work programme administrator. As a result of this concern it would be necessary to provide robust complaint procedures for those in the scheme.

Complaints would need to be investigated while the guaranteed work scheme continued, and so there would need to be well-planned suspension and investigation procedures. If one member of staff is accused then that member could be suspended while an investigation would be undertaken. During this period of suspension, others could take on the work of the suspended worker. If an entire team were accused of colluding to abuse or exploit workers, or commit any kind of fraud, then it would be necessary to respond in a more robust manner. These could perhaps involve an outside team taking over a local programme and to investigate the claims against the managers. The local managers would either be reinstated or would have to leave their posts as managers of the schemes.

Conclusion

In this chapter I have anticipated some of the concerns that people may have about the move to a system with hourly averaging, a comprehensive acquired income tax base, and a guaranteed work programme. The first set of concerns relate to the fear that the system would have detrimental economic consequences. I explained that the system would automatically counteract boom and bust cycles, and that the creation of a Sovereign Wealth Fund would abate the worry about overconsumption. This fund would need to have a degree of independence from the government and would have the brief that it should make investments with minimal political interference.

The remainder of the chapter explained the constitutional and institutional checks and balances that would be necessary to reduce the chance that governments and government agents would not be able to abuse their power. While governments would have greater potential power with the CLIPH-rate tax that does not mean that they would use it for nefarious purposes. Constitutional rules would need to be introduced and applied in order to ensure that individuals were not overpowered by the state and its agents. States should have the interests of all its citizens at heart, but the best designed constitutional rules do guarantee the proper treatment of all members of society. Many states have flouted their own rules, and so it is up to citizens to be vigilant about what their state does in their name and to protest against any failure to live up to the ideal that all members of society are owed security, respect, and freedom.

CHAPTER SEVEN
ANTI-FRAUD MEASURES

PERHAPS the most serious concern which I need to address is the concern that hourly averaging would be too vulnerable to fraud, and thus unfeasible. I have already discussed income fraud in chapter four, and some of the forms fraud currently available to unscrupulous individuals would continue to be available in a system with hourly averaging. However, hourly averaging creates an additional state institution that can be defrauded; hour credits. Criminals who obtain illicit hour credits without detection would gain not only the immediate money that these credits confer, but would also have a lower tax-rate for the remainder of their lives. I will therefore devote this chapter to the discussion of the anti-fraud measures that would need to be employed in a society with hourly averaging.

I will begin the chapter by setting the scene and the terms of the discussion. I will present useful categorisations that enable me to show that states should take a reasonably robust approach to fraud, though not an overly severe one. I will then explain how the rules regarding hour credits should be designed in order to block and discourage potential fraudsters. In the following section I will discuss the process of gathering information that will be used both to decide which employers and individuals should be further investigated and also to prosecute those who engage in fraud. The public will have a role to play in providing information and I will explain how members of the public would have access to some of the tax information on those about which they have suspicions. A well-designed computer system will help to focus investigative resources by cross-referencing to find suspicious individuals and employers.

Certain types of employer and employee are particularly troubling and I will devote a section to such cases. I will then give further information regarding the nature of the investigations that the tax compliance authorities can undertake to gather further information and prosecute those who commit hour credit fraud. I will end the chapter on a more positive note by highlighting some of the advantages that hour credits would bring about regarding fraud and other criminal activity.

Responding to fraud

In order to explain the appropriate response to fraud I will begin by distinguishing three different types of taxpayer or citizen. I will explain that the most appropriate strategies and responses to potential fraudsters differ depending upon which of these three types one is dealing with. This discussion will set the scene for the discussion of anti-fraud measures set out in the following sections of this chapter.

I will refer to the first type of taxpayer I will consider as the *rule-follower*. These individuals will follow the rules set by their society, irrespective of their potential ability to gain from flouting them and what anyone else does regarding these rules. People will follow rules because they always blindly follow rules and laws. More plausibly, some will follow rules because they feel they have a duty to follow the rules of their society if they have been set in a legitimate manner. Put differently, they follow legitimate rules because they are a good person who acts in accordance with their duties.

Rule-followers are of little interest to a discussion of fraud as they will not knowingly or intentionally commit fraud.

However, if it is possible to get people into this group then the proportion of fraud committed in society will decrease. Improving the attitudes of society towards correct taxpaying—as well as spreading information about the rules, expectations, and duties placed on taxpayers—may increase the numbers of people who believe in the importance of the rules and therefore follow them.

A second type of taxpayer is one who will follow rules if they think that others in society are also going to do so; the *conditional rule-follower*. Many people would accept that taxation benefits all of society and know they should do their bit by paying their correct share; they are good people in that regard. However, conditional rule-followers will not be inclined to pay their fair share if they feel other individuals are not doing so. This could be because they do not want to be taken as saps.[95] Second, it could be because they want to act in accordance with the norms of their society, and they feel that others do not have the positive norms.[96] Third, they might desire to follow legitimate rules but—mistakenly—feel that the rules are illegitimate; the reverse of a sub-group described above. Finally, they may desire to commit fraud because they have negative associations with the tax authorities, such as a feeling of distrust or victimisation.[97] If conditional rule-followers think that other people are free-riding then they will be tempted to do the same. However, if they feel that most other people are paying their fair share, and the government is using this money in an appropriate manner, then they will not utilise an opportunity to improve their position with regard to taxation.[98]

The third type of taxpayer I will distinguish is the *rational economic calculator*. Moral considerations have no bearing on such an individual, who will take any opportunity to free-ride if it is likely to benefit them materially. Of course, their attitude to risk will play a role in their decisions. Risk-lovers might be happy to take a large risk if the potential gain is large enough, while the risk-averse might not attempt to commit fraud unless there is a very low chance of being caught. Perhaps tellingly, this rational calculator is the individual imagined by mainstream (some might say "neoliberal") economists in their response to fraud and punishment.[99] Those who view everyone in this way therefore ignore the presence of the first and second groups when analysing issues of fraud, crime, and punishment.

The existence of the second and third types of individual creates the need for anti-fraud measures. Of course, in different societies and at different times, the relative size of these groups would vary, and so I will only talk in broad terms in this chapter. However, the point to emphasise is that the anti-fraud measures should focus on groups two and three. One approach is to try to "nudge" members of the third group into the second group and those in the second group into the first group.[100] This might happen gradually over the course of numerous generations. Aside from changing the relative sizes of the three groups mentioned above over time, the responses to fraud need to focus on the third group in order to increase the likelihood of compliance by the second group. If the likelihood that members of group three will successfully commit fraud is reduced, and if those in group three avoid publicly discussing their attempts at fraud, the members of the second group will comply with the rules. As a result, it may be sensible to put more resources into catching fraudsters than might be calculated if we simply compare the budgetary costs against the direct revenue gains of attacking tax fraud.

Nevertheless, it is necessary to be mindful of the costs of anti-fraud measures. The costs of ensuring total compliance would be huge, both in resources and the intrusion into everyone's lives that would be necessary in order to make fraud virtually impossible. The aim should therefore be to keep fraud to a minimum, even if it is fairly expensive to do so, but to accept that some fraud will still occur.

The anti-fraud measures focussed on members of the third group should have three components. The first component is that it should be made as difficult as possible for members of the third group to commit fraud in the first place. The opportunity for fraud should be limited where this can be done without too great a cost. Second, resources should be expended in order to uncover instances of fraud, reducing the chance that a fraudster will be successful. The third component is that there should be penalties for those caught committing fraud, for example that they should repay the amount defrauded and also face further penalties. This would act as a deterrent, given that potential fraudsters will weigh the prospective benefits against the prospective costs when considering whether to take an opportunity to commit fraud.

Undertaking the three components should reduce the likelihood that individuals of the third type will attempt fraud in the first place. If these individuals are simply rational calculators, then reducing the size of the potential benefit available, increasing the chance of uncovering their activity, and ensuring there are penalties for those who are convicted of fraud will change the attractiveness of the potential fraud. By rigging the calculations in this way many of those in the third group will not engage in large-scale fraud, which would reassure those in the second group that the system is working. In this chapter I will outline some of the methods that could be employed to ensure that members of group three would only be able to get away with very small scale frauds, if any at all. At the end of the chapter I will highlight some of the additional benefits that could arise as a result of combining the CLIPH-rate tax with thorough anti-fraud measures.

Rule setting

As fraud is such a worry for an economy with hour credits it is important to design the systems to make fraud difficult from the outset. One aspect of this is limiting the extent to which people can benefit from fraud. The second aspect is to create a system in which those who commit fraud stand to lose a large amount in order to provide a strong disincentive to those who might be tempted to engage in fraud. In this section I will outline some rules which would achieve these aims.

The first element of the system that would reduce the scope for fraud is what I will refer to as hard restrictions. These are rules, mentioned in chapter three on hour credits, which are built into the system which the taxation computer system will enforce automatically. The first restriction is the enforcement of a maximum number of hour credits that a worker can obtain in a given period, for example 42 hour credits a week. If anyone performs more work than this—which they are welcome to do without any penalty—they will not obtain any more hour credits than the maximum. This maximum will provide some reassurance to taxpayers that there is a limit on the amount that fraudsters can obtain illicitly. The risk of detection for a fraudster will rise as the amount of defrauded hour credits rises; someone claiming 42 hours for 40 hours work is much less likely to be caught than someone claiming 42 hours for 10 hours work. This means that fraudsters would tend to limit themselves to very small numbers of hour credits, the benefits of which may not then be worth the risk of being caught.

Another hard restriction I have mentioned previously is that limitations will be placed on employers who give out hour credits. Private employers would have to regularly show they are viable and well-funded businesses in order to retain their right to give out hour credits. Furthermore, the number of hour credits conferred should be linked to the turnover and profit of the business compared to rivals in the same industry. Businesses with sufficient profit would have little more to prove in order to have the right to confer hour credits. Some businesses make no profit as they are attempting to expand, in which case they would have to regularly show that they have sufficient funds to cover their costs in the upcoming period. It may be sensible to have a "warning list" of employers who appear to have financial woes or a dubious business model. These employers could be restricted such that their workers would initially receive a proportion (say, half) of the hour credits they have been allocated, with the other half withheld as temporary hour credits until the accounts for the firm are verified.

I have also mentioned a third hard restriction; a minimum gross hourly wage which would apply to certain employers at a higher rate than others. The highest rates would apply to political and religious groups, sports clubs, and those companies whose workers do what many people enjoy doing as a hobby. This is because many people would do these activities for free if they could afford to, and would relish the chance for a subsidised income in order to work for such employers.

Workers would receive hour credits into their tax account after the credits are submitted by their managers. Managers would log in to the tax authority system and input the hours worked (and other information such as the money paid). This means that managers would have a vitally important public role, a great responsibility that could be abused. Due to the importance of this role, I would suggest that managers should have to undertake some form of training before having the right to confer hour credits. In addition, managers should have to attend an event once a year which would culminate in a ceremony in which they would pledge allegiance to perform their public duties with integrity.

Conferring hour credits is vitally important for both managers and employers; if they lose this right then they lose all the financial and other benefits that go with it. The rules regarding hour credits therefore link to the third rule-based method of deterring hour credit fraud; providing a disincentive. Disincentives would exist by imposing fines on fraudsters. Furthermore, companies which commit hour credit fraud would be liable to pay fines. For companies engaging in widespread deception, the limit of the fines would be the transfer of the company and all its assets into state ownership for sale to its rival companies. This sets a strong incentive on company owners to place no pressure on managers to take risks to reduce their wage costs by colluding with workers to confer fraudulent hour credits.

The importance of the right to confer hour credits creates a strong incentive for individuals to behave in an honest and upright manner. Those who are convicted of hour credit fraud, and possibly other forms of fraud as well, would lose their right to hold important positions, such as a company director or a manager with the right to confer hour credits. This would bar fraudsters from important and remunerative positions for a specified period, harming their careers and finances. These disincentives for company owners and managers to engage in fraud should ensure that dishonest persons will only attempt hour credit fraud if they think they have little chance of getting caught. In the remainder of this chapter I will explain further steps that the anti-fraud authorities can take in order to increase the likelihood of catching fraudsters.

Information gathering

In order to catch fraudsters the anti-fraud authority needs to collect as much information as possible, which is thankfully feasible given advances in computer technology. This information can be used to indicate where to undertake more extensive investigations and to support prosecutions against fraudsters. I will discuss these uses of the information in later sections. For now I will outline some of the information that should be routinely gathered by the authorities, or which should be actively sought.

Hour credit fraud would involve collusion between managers and workers, and so information regarding this relationship may be useful. I would therefore suggest that all job advertisements should be registered with the tax authority, with the information about the type of job, the pay, and the expected hours. The anti-fraud authority can arrange for job seekers to report on job package negotiations, and could observe such interactions either using planted jobseekers or by clandestine observation of job package negotiations.

Employers would also have to provide copies of all current contracts with their employees, tracked to a job application where relevant. When employees change jobs within the employ of a particular employer the authorities would require a copy of this contract as well. This contract would contain details about the hour expectations of the job, and the pay for the job, including the regular hourly rate, overtime rate, and bonus entitlements, where relevant. Where companies promote internal candidates, managers would be asked to provide information about the nature of the new role. All workers would have their job role added to their account, such as lawyer, teacher, and so on. This would enable checks against other people with the same job type. Managers and workers would both also have to make a declaration whether the party other is known to them, and if so, the nature and source of that relationship. Lying about such a relationship would be a punishable offence.

A second source of information comes from tip-offs and evidence provided by individuals who suspect that an employee and manager are committing fraud. This information could come from several sources. One source is other public servants, who might have suspicions that individuals are involved in criminal activity. In the system I am describing, criminals would need to set up an illicit company in order to launder the proceeds of crime and confer hour credits in order to ensure that they were not guilty of income fraud. A second source would be that of whistle-blowers from within institutions with managers or owners engaged in suspicious activity. They may have raised their concerns about a rogue manager with higher managers and received a suspiciously inadequate response, or they may simply think it more appropriate to pass on information anonymously. Whistle-blowers should be provided the upmost legal protection and support to encourage the reporting of suspicious individuals.

A third source of further information is the local community. Indeed, there could be public media campaigns to encourage people to report suspicious people within their organisation or community. Some people may notice neighbours whose lifestyle does not appear to match their working hours and they could report their observations to the anti-fraud authorities. This might be an indication of hour credit fraud, income fraud, or simply a mistake on the part of the observer. In order to reduce the scope for such mistakes I would suggest that people should be able to access tax information on individuals known to them. This information would include lifetime totals of hour credits, gross income from earned and unearned sources, and net income. These figures would also be provided for a recent period as well. The information provided could also indicate any convictions and fines the taxpayer has received, and the names of their manager and any workers. This limited information might be enough to allay suspicions, but it might not.

Only tax-fraud investigation officers would have access to the *full* and detailed information about individual taxpayers, for privacy reasons. Furthermore, even other state investigators—such as police officers—should only have access to the limited information unless they obtain a warrant or some kind of judicial approval. Nevertheless, the police and the general public should be able to discover the above mentioned information on named taxpayers, or taxpayers at a named address, which should be enough to indicate whether the person really is living beyond their legally obtained means.

A final source of information that I will mention here is that of regular audits of all employers. Teams of assessors and auditors would investigate every company on a scheduled basis. They would assess the accounts of the company, and compare these to the activity of the company and a physical inspection of the business in action. The assessors could check multiple things at once, such as compliance with accounting and regulatory practice, and checking for income fraud as well as hour credit fraud. After all, companies acting as fronts for criminal enterprises will engage in several of these activities at once. The issue relevant to this chapter is that of hour credit fraud, and the assessors would check whether employees are performing the work expected of them. Assessors would know the structure of the organisation as they can map this structure with the hour credit information they have. This information will show who manages whom and how much each of these workers obtains per hour. As well as intensive audits as required—perhaps depending on the industry and company in question—the anti-fraud teams would undertake unannounced spot checks and also pose as potential customers to discover whether the business is really engaging in the activity it claims to be. Employers which raise the suspicions of auditors would be subject to further investigations and checks.

Computer-based checks

Another branch of the anti-fraud authorities would be computer-based. This branch would cross-reference information to check for suspicious patterns. Tax and benefit authorities are already undertaking such cross-referencing to ensure that benefit claimants are not also paying taxes, which would indicate they are fraudulent or mistaken claimants. These checks would be more straightforward where the benefit and tax system are combined together and where there is a maximum weekly hour credit claim. In this section I will outline some of the additional checks that can be utilised to highlight potential fraudsters.

I have said that all current contract information should be known to the tax authority. A simple automatic check is simply whether the amount paid to the worker matches an amount that corresponds to the contract given and the number of hour credits claimed. The system could account for the different rates that people may earn, for example overtime and public holiday rates.[101]

Illicit contracts will be harder to uncover where workers change their role within a company, as they may take the opportunity to collude and write a false contract. This kind of activity is more likely to be picked up by a second check. This is to search for workers who receive a decrease in their hourly wage, or at least do not receive an increase when their job changes substantially. These cases could be brought to the attention of the investigative branch. Most will no doubt be perfectly innocent, but investigating such cases will provide greater compliance and reassurance to law-abiding taxpayers.

In the previous section I also indicated that managers should include with the contract information a job description and a listing of job-type. This information can also be used to indicate workers who earn a lower hourly amount than others performing the same or similar work in the same market. In some cases such differences may be innocent, but this information might be useful in indicating individuals and companies who should receive extra attention from the anti-fraud authorities. It could trigger an investigation into a company or the individual in question, or the information could be recorded and taken into account at the next comprehensive audit.

The computer system could also utilise databases to check whether workers and managers might be known to one another even if they have not indicated as such. This could be done by collecting information from birth certification and the records of gifts made in order to create a virtual map of connections between individuals.[102] Workers and managers could be checked against this virtual map in order to uncover connections that have not been admitted by the parties involved.

As well as cross-referencing workers, it is possible to cross-reference managers and whole companies. Managers who have an unusually low average gross hourly rate or an unusually large number of staff can be flagged up by the system for further investigation either as a priority or at the next audit. Companies, or their constituent sub-parts in the case of large conglomerations, could be compared with their rivals in the same industry. Companies that pay less per hour than their rivals or whose management structure appears very different could be flagged up.

I have given just a few examples of the kinds of checks that computers can perform relatively cheaply in order to turn large amounts of information into useful indicators. More complicated checks might be even more pinpointed, perhaps developed as time goes on and more and more fraudulent operations are uncovered. The cross referencing will not catch all fraudsters, of course. However, it will direct investigative resources towards those who are most suspicious. This means that those who wish to engage in fraud will have to limit their hour credit fraud to very small amounts in order to avoid raising suspicions. This should increase everyone's trust in the system.

Employers and employees of particular concern

I have indicated what information should be available to the anti-fraud authorities and the kinds of computer-based cross referencing that can alert these authorities to suspicious cases. These will help to uncover hour credit fraud. Nevertheless, certain kinds of employers and employees present particular difficulties to the reliability of the hour credit system. In this section I will outline these cases and indicate how to respond to them.

Traditionally, businesses which primarily deal in cash have been the most troubling regarding fraud. Cash is difficult to track and easy to use, and therefore highly popular with criminal enterprises. Some businesses providing legitimate services may use their cash in order to provide their workers with illicit payments that circumvent taxation. This is a form of income fraud, which I discussed briefly in chapter four, and it would be attacked with the usual methods; for example surreptitiously observing the cash handling processes of the business. So-called "cash-in-hand" fraud is less likely to be an issue where there is progressive hourly averaging. Most workers who receive illicit payments are low-paid and so workers and their employers will have a strong incentive to legitimise their businesses and provide thorough accounts in order to qualify for the right to confer hour credits.

The highly progressive taxation proposed as part of hourly averaging, on the other hand, creates more of a temptation for those with high hourly incomes to seek to evade taxation. Employers which can find ways to remunerate their highly valuable staff in ways that circumvent detection, will have an advantage over their rivals. Furthermore, employees have a clear incentive to want to obtain tax-free rather than highly-taxed income. The anti-fraud authorities would therefore need to pay special attention to those who will have the greatest to benefit from such income fraud. While this is not, again, a form of hour credit fraud it is something for the authorities to check for in their audits and activities. Employers might be tempted to provide perks for their valuable staff which are difficult to detect, such as luxury surroundings. Companies which provide services which can enhance the lives of workers in other companies should therefore receive additional focus from anti-fraud investigations, and the goods they provide to other employers should also be subject to particular scrutiny.

I said in chapter one that the main test of the legitimacy of a company is that it can obtain private investment to fund its operations. However, this may create a loophole by which people in powerful positions in business can benefit their loved ones. It is possible to imagine someone who has built up a business who would not be able to pass on the resources of the business without facing significant taxation on their own gains and also significant taxation on the gift to the loved ones. They may instead be tempted to set up a subsidiary which employs benefactors with little requirements that the subsidiary makes any money. Alternatively, their loved ones could set up a business and obtain funding from their benefactor's business group. The anti-fraud computer systems would need to search for situations of these kinds, and auditors would need to be alert to the possibility, particularly regarding companies who seem to secure funding without having any obvious revenues or products.

Perhaps the most troubling issue regarding hour-credit fraud is the case of workers who are their own managers—namely the *self-employed*. As these people supervise themselves it is more difficult to make checks on their self-supervision. There is no manager-worker relationship which can provide reassurance regarding work activity, given the incentives that managers have to make full use of their staff. Self-employed people might be considered, without any further investigations, to only need to do the minimum amount work required in order to claim the maximum hour credits for their business activities. Of course, many self-employed workers would want to do more than this for many reasons; such as their desire to grow their business, their enjoyment of their work, their sense of social duty, or simply in order to increase their gross and therefore net income. Nevertheless, the worry that a significant number of self-employed workers would be tempted to overstate their hours worked is such that additional requirements should be made on those who request the right to self-certify their hour credits.

The self-employed will face close scrutiny from the tax and anti-fraud authorities, and it must be emphasised that these activities should be undertaken in a sensitive and understanding manner. Requests for information from the self-employed, and others flagged up for greater scrutiny, should be prefaced by apologies and explanations. These should explain that they face greater scrutiny because their work is one that would attract fraudsters, and so the legitimate businesses have to distinguish themselves from the fraudsters. After all, it is legitimate to place greater emphasis on investigating the self-employed and those in certain industries, as they hold positions into which fraudsters would self-select themselves.

I have hinted at some features that are immediately helpful at reducing fraud by the self-employed. The first is the imposition of an hour credit maximum, which limits the range of hours that the self-employed can "steal." The lower limit on this range is provided by the requirement that businesses need to be sufficiently successful in order to qualify for hour credits in the first place. These requirements could be higher for the self-employed, varying in line with the nature of the work. So someone who is self-employed, as their industry generally involves freelance work, may need to have a turnover above that of £10 per hour credit. Meanwhile, someone who is self-employed as they have a highly desired skill, may be required to have a turnover of £1,000 per hour credit. The temptation for the highly skilled to leave regular employment and become self-employed in order to obtain greater leisure would thereby be reduced. Much attention would need to be paid to these self-employed enterprises in order to ensure that the minimum turnover required is appropriate given any potential changes in market conditions.

Self-employed worker-manager-owners would also have to provide a greater amount of information on working hours than regular employers and employees. This would be more onerous on such enterprises, which produces another disincentive to undertake work in this capacity when it is possible to perform the work as part of an enterprise. Nevertheless, one form of compensation for this additional work is that these activities would qualify as work for the purposes of hour credits. The information that self-employed workers would need to provide could take the form of a diary of their work activities under different headings, along with proof that the listed activities were undertaken. Enterprising industries could create machines or computer apps that would enable workers to record this information with ease. The addition of copies of emails sent to clients, work completed, and work bid for would be sufficient to supplement most applications. Those who provide more evidence would be less likely to face more intensive audits.

The anti-fraud authorities can follow up these submissions by asking alleged clients and suppliers whether they have had the dealings with the self-employed person in question and how long they might expect such work to take. The authorities could pose as potential clients or suppliers in order to check that the business is as active as its owner claims it to be. By limiting the hour credits available to self-employed workers, requiring the additional information of them, and making greater checks and investigations on them, it should be possible to be reasonably sure that the self-employed are working as many hours as they claim.

Investigations and prosecutions

At several points in this chapter I have described indicators that would trigger more intensive investigation, which would lead towards the prosecution of those who engage in hour credit fraud. In this section I will briefly discuss these crucial points.

I have listed several factors that would greatly increase the—otherwise random and relatively low—chance that a taxpayer or employer would face investigation beyond an occasional audit. One is the receipt of a tip-off from a member of the public or a whistle-blower within an organisation. Other triggers for investigation would be that workers and managers are

known to one another. Anti-fraud officers and other important officials may also expect greater investigation due to their
potential to protect fraudsters from prosecution, whether for
personal reasons or out of corruption. Employers in certain
industries and the self-employed would also face greater scrutiny and covert information gathering than other employers.
Finally, the computer system will be designed to focus investigations on taxpayers and companies who have suspicious
earnings patterns.

I have already indicated what these further investigations
may involve. One is that investigators—or those contracted by
them—could pose as customers, clients, and job applicants to
see if the company engages in any outwardly fraudulent behaviour and to collect further information about the business.
These activities would be undertaken for all employers anyway,
but could be particularly focussed on businesses deemed more
suspicious. This would be supplemented by familiar investigative approaches such as covertly monitoring individuals or
business premises.

The aim of these investigations is to supplement any evidence
already gathered on the suspect in order to secure a successful prosecution of hour credit fraud—as well as income fraud
where both occur together. Employers and taxpayers would be
asked to make regular declarations and statements to the relevant authorities and if the evidence gathered contradicts these
declarations then this would be sufficient to prosecute the
taxpayer. In some cases the evidence received from audits and
other information—such as evidence that someone was away
on holiday when they were claiming hour credits for working—might be sufficient to prosecute, but I imagine in many
cases the information gathered automatically would need
to be supplemented by surveillance information or witness
testimony.

Advantages of hour credits and acquired income

It may be clear from what I have said in this chapter and in chapter four that enforcing the CLIPH-rate tax would involve more intensive anti-fraud activity than the existing system. This would be reasonably expensive, even though intelligent use of computer power should make these activities more efficient than they might otherwise be. Fortunately, using hour credits and the acquired income tax base would have several compensating benefits regarding criminal activity and social cohesion, and I will end this chapter by emphasising these advantages.

It is impossible to know the size of the "black-market" or "shadow economy," but estimates have indicated it is somewhere between 18.5% and 27% of the worldwide economy. In more developed countries it is slightly lower, but still 14% to 22%.[103] It is useful to take this into account when considering the case for hour credits and an acquired income tax-base with publicly available information and strong accountancy principles. I would suggest that hourly averaging would greatly interrupt a lot of illicit economic activity, firstly because criminal enterprises would need to launder money and hour credits through legitimate-seeming businesses. Creating these quasi-legitimate businesses and avoiding suspicion—despite the evidence that could so easily be presented regarding the activities of their employees and true products—would take a large amount of planning and resources. This would reduce the profitability of such enterprises while increasing the chance of detection. Furthermore, remembering that Al Capone was only ever convicted of tax evasion, the CLIPH-rate tax offers much improved chances of catching those who engage in large-scale criminal activity for gain.

A second point regarding the shadow economy is to emphasise the incentives created by hour credits. Hour credits are very valuable to their owners, since they both represent immediate income and also last for the lifetime of the taxpayer. The desire for hour credits should therefore push many "hard-to-tax"[104] workers and small enterprises who might be tempted to work "cash-in-hand" or who might not insist that their employers fully register their employment to ensure that their work is appropriately accredited. This would push people towards the legitimate economy. Another way to put the above two points is that hour credits make legitimate work pay to a greater extent while reducing the benefits from criminal work. The CLIPH-rate tax would push the economy as a whole towards more legitimate enterprise, and while this would not eliminate the shadow economy, it should reduce it substantially. In this way the move towards the acquired income tax-base and hourly averaging would together provide incentives for people to organise their working arrangements in ways that would make fraudulent behaviour more apparent.

A further advantage of the CLIPH-rate tax is that I imagine it would increase the likelihood that people would choose to contribute to society and to pay the correct amount of taxation. As I explained at the start of this chapter, if conditional rule-followers feel that there is a strong social norm that people should report their true income and hour credits, then they will not make use of any opportunities they have to commit fraud. There are several reasons to think this shift in norms would occur. The first is that the CLIPH-rate tax would only be introduced after many years of strong advocacy by a large majority of society. This advocacy would be a strong social signal that the proposed system is desirable and that people wish to live in accordance with it.

I will also propose a second, slightly more speculative, reason for thinking that the norms of a CLIPH-rate tax society would make people less likely to commit fraud; that such a society would have greater solidarity than other capitalist systems would engender. One way this would occur is because hour credits allow people with varying skills and talents to have a comparable measure of their contribution to society. In other capitalist societies, gross income can be too readily taken to be the only indication that someone has performed valuable work. However, hour credits can also indicate that someone has contributed to society and this information would be publicly available. Hopefully those who have lower gross incomes would have a greater feeling that they are making a contribution to society through their work, and that this contribution would also be appreciated by the rest of society.

Another, related, argument stems from the fact that that the hourly tax system ties the income of all members of society together. As a result, people should feel a greater economic affinity to the rest of their society. The differences in economic class should be much less apparent, and therefore the society should be less stratified, with people mixing more with those from other economic groups. The differences in actual economic class would be less outwardly obvious. Furthermore, it would be more difficult to drive artificial—nonsensical—distinctions between people, such as that between public and private sector workers and that between "strivers" and "skyvers" in recent tabloid and political debates in the UK. The guaranteed job scheme and negative tax-rates would reassure people that those who obtain public subsidy will not be undeserving recipients. The CLIPH-rate tax society should have much less hostility between the interests of different classes which should improve the norms and togetherness of the society. This in turn would improve the honesty of taxpayers and companies.

Conclusion

In this chapter I have explained what steps would be necessary in order to ensure reliable compliance with the hour credit system. This consists of a mixture of information gathering and enforcement techniques which would increase the confidence of decent taxpayers that others are not defrauding the rest of their society. When added to the increased confidence in compliance and feelings of solidarity that I predict for a CLIPH-rate tax society, most taxpayers will act in an honest way in their dealings with the tax authorities.

I will end with a recap of the methods I have described which would be used to detect and prosecute hour credit fraud. Of course, these were only indicative and are not intended to be exhaustive. I began by emphasising that the rules of the system would be designed from the start in such a way that fraud would be difficult. This would include the mandatory collection of information on employers and taxpayers which would be useful in detecting those 1) who are more likely to be in a position to abuse the system and 2) whose activities most arouse suspicion. This would involve the use of a computer system that would point investigators to the most likely abusers; those who employ people who they know personally, those with valuable skills, and the self-employed. Investigative resources would therefore be required to monitor such employers and employees in order to ensure that people trust in the integrity of the system. As long as this trust is maintained the vast majority of taxpayers are likely to desire to declare the correct amount of hour credits. I have speculated that over time a CLIPH-rate tax society is likely to generate greater solidarity, trust, and fidelity. This would in turn increase the efficiency of the society, which may even outweigh any of the additional costs of anti-fraud measures. Even if this hunch is incorrect and the advantages of the CLIPH-rate tax would not offset the costs, then the advantage of living in a more just and equitable society still clearly outweighs the cost of additional anti-fraud investigators.

CHAPTER EIGHT

TRANSITIONAL CONDITIONS

IMAGINE a society in which the majority of citizens clearly wish to introduce the hourly averaging proposals I described in the first two parts of this book. A small movement of committed individuals advocated the system and eventually all the major political parties have come to support the proposal. Unfortunately a clear mandate and some political will to introduce the system would not be sufficient in order for it to work. Certain conditions would need to be met in order for the system to work effectively. In this chapter I will discuss the steps that would need to be taken before our imagined society could make the transition to the CLIPH-rate tax.

The first issue I will discuss is the international ecology in which a state with hourly averaging could survive. Many international structures, such as those existing at the present time, would not be favourable to a single state wishing to introduce hourly averaging. This is because the tax and capital competition from non-hourly states would undermine the system by drawing highly paid workers and business ownership away from the state with hourly averaging. However, there are several international ecosystems in which a state could effectively enforce the CLIPH-rate tax and I will describe some of these.

In the second half of the chapter I will discuss the internal conditions that would be necessary prior to the introduction of the CLIPH-rate tax. The tax authority would need a certain amount of time to prepare its systems and would need to collect certain information. I will explain the processes of information gathering that the authorities would need to undertake and the options available when transitioning from annual to lifetime taxation.

International tax competition

Taxation proposals that increase taxes on some taxpayers—such as the proposals in this book—always receive the complaint that they would reduce the "tax competitiveness" of the state compared to others. In this section I will explain this complaint and the related issue of competitive tax avoidance. I will end by outlining a related issue; competitive tax avoidance.

The issue of international tax competition arises where states can attempt to poach workers or investment on the basis of their lower taxation. The first of these issues is also known as talent flight or the brain drain. Of course, states may lose talented individuals to others for other reasons than tax competitiveness, such as the gross pay differentials or improved quality of life in the more attractive state. Indeed, some have therefore suggested that tax competition does not occur as these other factors are so much more important[105]. However, I will assume that the prospect of a lower tax bill may conceivably tempt some workers to move state.

As well as competition for workers, states also compete for capital investment. Firms may be able to locate themselves in several different states in order to cover a particular market, and the total amount of tax rate they will have to pay will be one factor firms will take into account. Firms will consider this factor along with many others such as the infrastructure of the state and the skills and costs of the workers available to them.

Some thinkers believe that these forms of tax competition are a good thing. One reason given is because it gives people a choice of states with different levels of tax and spending.[106]

This is a problematic line of argument, however, since people with different needs will "prefer" different levels of spending for reasons they cannot help; someone with a severe disability would be better off in a higher tax state, while someone who can earn large amounts of money would be better off in a lower tax state. Others have suggested that without tax competition, states would all tend to increase their taxes and would become leviathans which will overtax their citizens, as I discussed in chapter six. The third reason comes from those who hold a theory of distributive justice that is against most forms of taxation, i.e. libertarianism.[107] I am not convinced by any of these arguments, as should be clear from comments made at various stages in this book.

The downside of tax competition is the concern for the introduction of the CLIPH-rate tax. This is the worry that tax competition leads to a race-to-the-bottom, whereby states cannot raise taxation above a certain point because the costs would be too high. This concern applies strongly to the CLIPH-rate tax as it is explicitly designed to tax incomes to the highly talented and investors at a much higher rate than other tax systems. In a world of race-to-the-bottom tax competition, CLIPH-rate tax states may struggle if investors, entrepreneurs, and skilled workers relocate to non-CLIPH-rate tax states where they can earn a higher net income. As a consequence, CLIPH-rate tax states may find it hard to compete economically and their citizens may become poorer than those of other states as time goes on. In the first part of this chapter I will discuss the possible responses to tax competition.

However, before presenting international tax ecosystems that would enable the CLIPH-rate tax, I will explain the important relationship between international tax competition and international tax avoidance. The cases of tax competition I gave above made reference to the total amount of tax that mobile taxpayers would have to pay in different states. This is partly about tax rates, but the tax base is a crucial factor as well. States can offer investors and foreign nationals special tax breaks in order to coax them, an invidious practice that is explicitly designed to steal the tax base from other states. A similarly predatory and parasitic activity is undertaken by states who offer wealthy individuals and companies the opportunity to hide their income from the tax authorities of the states that would otherwise tax them. These small states are often called "tax havens," but should more accurately be called secrecy jurisdictions as it is secrecy that they offer via their financial institutions. These states attract investment funds, but the investments are not really made there. Secrecy jurisdictions merely hide the owners of investments made elsewhere, so that the wealthy investors can avoid—or more accurately evade—taxation.

These activities should be clamped down upon through international agreements as they make truly progressive taxation much less effective by allowing members of the super-rich global elite to escape taxation on their gains—whether ill-gotten or legitimate. This would involve greater cooperation between states to share information and to support one another in the taxation of their citizens. The practice of states offering special tax treatment for foreign nationals should also be stopped.

Compatible international ecosystems

In this section I will present some international ecosystems which would enable a state to introduce the CLIPH-rate tax. These compatible ecosystems are not necessarily attractive, and I will begin with the least attractive of the compatible systems. The ecosystems become gradually more attractive and in the following section I will describe the ideal situation. This is a world with numerous states which each have compatible CLIPH-rate tax systems with their own preferred tax rates, but which enables individuals who move between the various states to have a consistent and fair global lifetime tax calculation.

The first CLIPH-rate tax compatible global ecosystem I will describe is that of a single worldwide state. If such a state were to introduce hourly averaging it would face no competition from outside, since there would be no other state with an incompatible or hostile tax regime. However, while the creation of a global state would therefore remove this international barrier to the introduction of hourly averaging, it is difficult to consider it a positive option when all things are considered. Humans are social, cultural, and political animals; a human planted into alien human culture would struggle to deal with his new cultural environment to a much greater degree than any other animal would with members of its own species. It is hard to imagine how a state built on multiple languages and cultures could function effectively, certainly without overruling the views of the vast majority of its citizens. Such a state would therefore alienate the vast majority of its citizens, and fail to compel any allegiance from its members. A global state would no doubt need to rule by force rather than consent and would suffer from the risk of descending into tyranny and corruption. Such a state would not engender any solidarity or fellow feeling between its citizens, and this would also increase the likelihood of large scale fraud.

For these reasons, I do not think the human race is yet ready to have a single global state. Furthermore, if such a state would require the—increased—loss of the diversity of human cultures then it would not be a worthwhile undertaking. Some kind of federal state may avoid the worst of these fears and may be one way to express the ideal system I will describe in the following section. However, it would not be a good idea for a single central state apparatus to have sole access to police, military, and intelligence services; such a concentration of power would be an enticing opportunity for an individual or a group with a lust for power.

The opposite extreme is for a single state, or group of states, to *isolate* themselves economically from states with incompatible tax systems. If such a state or group of states had a sufficiently large internal market and a full range of natural resources then such isolation would be open to them. There are two problems with this approach, however. The first is that the states might not be able to fully isolate themselves from the rest of the global economy, particularly since some talented and ambitious individuals will always be tempted to leave for more personally lucrative shores. The second problem is that two separate economies will almost certainly be less efficient than they would be if they were combined; they will not get the benefits of those items that are cheaper across the border and they will lose out on the efficiencies of economies of scale.

A more benign version of the divided world ecosystem is a third possibility. This world is one in which there are non-hourly-averaging states, but these states agree not to undermine the hourly-averaging states. This would occur if the non-averaging states agreed to limit the extent to which individuals could benefit by leaving the hourly averaging societies. They could do this by enforcing the controls on capital movement imposed by hourly states and actively preventing individuals from illicitly gaining from investments made in states with hourly-averaging. The supportive non-hourly states would also share information regarding immigrants from hourly-averaging states and collecting taxation revenues on exiles from hourly-averaging at similar rates to that which would have fallen in the hourly-averaging states.

This benign solution faces several practical difficulties. States are currently likely to compete on taxation and attempt to attract workers and capital to their shores with low tax and promises of secrecy. It would be possible for hourly-averaging states to put sufficient pressure on non-averaging states, however, if they maintain a sufficient proportion of global economic activity and resources. If the hourly-averaging states were dominant, then they could insist that the non-hourly states rendered themselves compatible with their systems in order to have access to the global resources and markets. There are then two routes to a benign divided world solution for hourly averaging; either power and pressure, or the simple goodwill of non-averaging states. In the following section I will present the ideal global ecosystem for the implementation of the CLIPH-rate tax.

The ideal ecosystem: fair global taxation

In this section I will describe what I take to be the ideal international system. This is a world in which there are separate states which all have their own CLIPH-rate tax system, but at which they can choose their own rates. However, such a system would appear to engender tax competition, which was the problem with which we started. One option would be to constrain states in their ability to set tax-rates below those of other states in order to capture their capital or workers.[108] However, tax competition is not a bad thing if it does not undermine fair taxation within states. I therefore propose a system in which there is a counter-incentive for states to avoid the race-to-the-bottom in tax-rates.

The proposal I discuss here assumes that the acquired comprehensive income tax base would be applied universally throughout the world.[109] If this were the case then it would be possible to remove corporation taxation. At present a lot of tax avoidance comes through corporations using their multi-national status to shift their profits to low-tax jurisdictions, thus avoiding taxation in the places where their workers and customers are. If a comprehensive acquired income approach were not introduced globally then it would still be necessary to do something to stop the loss of tax revenue to corporations who engage in these, and other, tax avoiding practices.

If all states were to introduce a suitably similar *type* of tax system—the form of tax base and calculation—then it should be possible to create a system which would include a counter-incentive for states to reward those with higher tax-rates, and to stop the loss of tax revenues to lower-tax states. In addition, the system I describe in this section does not restrict the tax-rates that states can apply. The counter-incentive system works by focussing on individual taxpayers who have relationships with more than one state. These taxpayers would have a single global lifetime tax account. There is therefore a degree of similarity between single-nation taxpayers who simply pay the lifetime tax-rate of their state and multiple-nation taxpayers who have a more complex calculation. I will describe this calculation below.

Individuals who spend their entire lives within a single state have a relatively straightforward relationship with their state and fellow citizens. However, some individuals will have a relationship with several states, perhaps being born in one, having citizenship of another, growing up in a third, going to university in a fourth, working in a fifth, and retiring in a sixth. This individual has a relationship with at least six states—and possibly more if they have economic ties to further states. My suggestion for international taxation would take account of these relationships, and hold people to their past relationships. States could agree on a weighting of these various issues such that an international individual can have their relationship proportioned out between the various states with which they have had a relationship over their lifetime. I will not specify how such a relationship should be calculated, but will specify—implausibly—an individual who has a perfectly equal six-way relationship between the states mentioned above. Let us call this person Rachel.

As an international individual, Rachel would have a global tax-rate which would supersede the taxation she would pay in each state. Her global taxation would be collected either by an International Tax Organisation (ITO) or by a lead state which would collect information from the others. The ITO or lead state would calculate Rachel's global tax and then apportion the revenue out to the states with which she has had a relationship. I will describe the steps in this process.

The first step would be to calculate Rachel's lifetime global tax-rate. In order to do this the ITO or lead state would need to calculate how much tax Rachel would have paid on her global income if, counterfactually, she were a single-nation individual in each state respectively. Let us say she would have paid around 50% tax in four of the states (A, B, C, and D) and around 32% in two of the states (E and F). Her average tax-rate between these would be 44%, and so this should be her global tax-rate. The states would work together, via the ITO or the lead state, in order to ensure that she has paid the correct amount in global tax.

The second step is to apportion the revenue between these states. This is where the counter-incentive comes in. In order to reward states for setting higher tax-rates and penalise states who attempt to lure people with lower tax-rates, the revenue from each individual would not be allotted in accordance with the strength of their relationship with the various states. Instead, it would be weighted towards those states that would have taxed the citizen at a higher rate. So the revenue from Sarah's taxation would not be split evenly six ways between states A-F. Instead, states A-D would share perhaps 22% each with states E and F receiving 6% each.

If this system were actively enforced by all states then it would be an effective brake on tax competition. States would not be able to offer preferential tax-rates to foreigners, since the tax-rate on international citizens would be calculated based upon the tax-rates that would apply to their own nationals. This means that states would have to drop their tax-rates across the board, and thereby increase the subsidy paid to low-paid members of society. This expenditure on negative tax payments would require revenue, and would thus be difficult to fund from the counter-weighted income from international citizens. However, this system would still allow for some tax competition. States might gain from dropping their tax-rates below those of others, in terms of the additional revenue they could obtain. This would place an additional limit on any tendency that a state might have to maximise its revenues as much as possible, an issue I discussed in chapter six. A final advantage of this system is that international citizens would not be able to escape their relationships with their fellow-citizens from the past, since taxation would be calculated on a lifetime basis while taking account of these past relationships.

One worry that may arise is that states would not be trusted to enforce the taxes on multi-national citizens, since much of the revenue generated would go elsewhere. However, there are several factors that would count against this. Firstly, states will always have a financial incentive to uncover any income that occurs within their borders. They will obtain income from doing so for the remainder of the life of the taxpayer, both directly as part of the tax calculation and because it would increase the relationship that the taxpayer has with the state in question and thereby decrease the relationship—and payments—to the other states. Second, the ITO could operate relatively independently within each state. It could be staffed by workers from other states, who would assist and assess the local tax authority in their attempts to accurately tax both national and international citizens.

In briefly describing this proposal I have assumed that all the states in the world would agree to adopt the same tax base and to submit to an International Tax Organisation. This may appear overly idealistic. For example, why would 'tax haven' states agree to join such a system, since they would lose out on the advantages this status offers them? However, the proposal made above could be seen as an end goal that would guide the development of international taxation. It is possible to envisage a road map to such an end goal, the latter stages of which would allow the introduction of the CLIPH-rate in favourable states.

If there were a sufficiently powerful group of states with a desire to introduce the CLIPH-rate tax then they could create a grouping which could have relations of one of two types with other states. There would be those states which would not currently implement the CLIPH-rate tax, but which would agree to share taxation information, work with the CLIPH-rate tax states to block transfers that seek to avoid taxation, and to enforce taxation of immigrants from CLIPH-rate tax states at the same rates that would have been applied on them if they had not left. In exchange for these privileges, the *helpful states* would be able to trade with the CLIPH-rate tax states and receive other forms of assistance from them for as long as they actively assisted CLIPH-rate tax states in discouraging tax avoidance and evasion. Helpful states might not be expected to share the full revenue from CLIPH-rate tax immigrants; they would mainly be tasked with applying the tax-rates in order to reduce the tax incentives for people to leave a CLIPH-rate tax system.

Intransigent states, however, would be treated less favourably by the CLIPH-rate tax states. Intransigent states would not be allowed to trade with the CLIPH-rate tax states—except perhaps under strict conditions—and they may face further sanctions up to and including blockades if they should seek to poach workers and resources from CLIPH-rate tax states by offering lower tax-rates. Tax havens are of course parasitic on the markets of larger states, and so if intransigent states were cut off from such markets they would have nothing further to gain from being tax havens. It is important to note that states which were previously tax havens would not simply be coerced or punished into submission, however. Joining the international tax system would allow them to legitimately access to any unclaimed assets held by their financial institutions, which they could place in their sovereign wealth fund and use to benefit their citizens. Intransigent states which were not tax havens would be less amenable to the influence of CLIPH-rate tax states, of course, and it would be more difficult to have a stable international system with CLIPH-rate tax states if there were a very powerful group of intransigent states.

The above discussion shows that it might be possible to introduce the CLIPH-rate tax in some states even in the absence of global agreement. This would be possible as long as the other powerful states were willing to support the tax systems of CLIPH-rate tax states by collecting and sharing the relevant information on immigrants from CLIPH-rate tax states and by holding those individuals to the tax-rates that they would have paid if they had not left. CLIPH-rate tax states would put pressure on intransigent states to become helpful ones, and hope that helpful states will join the CLIPH-rate tax system and join the ITO system described above. Eventually, it would be hoped that all states would end up introducing the system.

In conclusion, the ideal international system is one in which states work together to tax individuals on their global income. States would agree to share the information and revenue for international citizens in exchange for being part of the international fair tax and trade system. I have also shown that it would be possible to introduce this system on a non-global level. Indeed, it seems more realistic that the states particularly keen to introduce the CLIPH-rate tax could create their own system initially, with other helpful states supporting it even if they do not join and intransigent states facing exclusion and hostility from CLIPH-rate tax states. Eventually, it would be hoped that all non-CLIPH-rate tax states would become helpful rather than intransigent and then fully join the system.

Practicalities of transition: Setting up the systems

Having discussed the international conditions required before our state could feasibly introduce the CLIPH-rate tax within its borders, I will now discuss the *internal* processes the state would need to undertake during the international discussions and negotiations, in order to be ready to introduce the system. In this section I will explain the broad stages that would apply in order to set up the discussion of the system changes and information required. In the following section, I will describe the new institutions and alterations to existing institutions that would be required. In the final section, I will describe the possibilities available to include information and tax from the previous non-hourly system.

In order to consider the issues of transitioning to hourly averaging, it is useful to distinguish three distinct periods, the middle of which is pertinent to this discussion. The first period is whatever overall tax system is in place prior to the introduction of hourly averaging. The third period is the running of the full hourly averaging system. The middle period is one in which various steps will be taken to move from the pre-existing system to hourly-averaging. This middle period can be subdivided into further stages.

The middle period begins when the first step on the way to the CLIPH-rate tax is introduced. This could be any constitutional amendments required, the introduction of legislation that sets the institutional changes and informational requirements in motion. We can refer to this middle period as one in which the two systems are in some sense *in parallel*, or *overlapping*. The overlapping period would begin with information gathering and some temporary tax policies designed to ease into the introduction of hourly averaging. These temporary taxes will eventually give way to the full-blown hourly system at the date set out in the initial legislation, or upon the meeting of the conditions set down in that legislation.

During the overlapping period a new taxation computer system would need to be introduced, though of course it can be fully designed beforehand. This system would be designed to be compatible with both the pre-existing and future taxation and benefit payment systems. In addition, states would work with each other to ensure the compatibility needed for the automatic—timely and accurate—taxation of international individuals by all the relevant states. The systems would be made in such a way that they can be switched from one form of calculation to another without any interruption.

Another activity that could take place during the middle period, and which could begin long before then, would be to gather information regarding the nature of different types of employment. In some cases this would be straightforward information about hourly pay and job satisfaction levels. However, it would be particularly important to get information on self-employed workers. By finding out how self-employed workers allocate their time and their expenses it will make it easier to assess their claims for hour credits once they are introduced. A further point on this subject is that hour credits could be utilised prior to the full introduction of hourly averaging so that managers get used to interacting with the system.

New and altered institutions

I will now describe some of the institutions that would need to be created or altered in order to facilitate the CLIPH-rate tax. I mentioned one of these in the previous section; that some temporary taxes might be necessary to stop the loss of the tax base prior to the introduction of the new system. Some people may attempt to alter their investment portfolios or make gifts earlier than planned once states begin the shift to a new system. Taxes would either discourage such activity, or provide a backstop source of revenue from those who would still engage in activities that would be taxed differently after the introduction of hourly averaging.

The majority of the new institutions that would assist in the accurate calculation of the CLIPH-rate tax would take the form of registries that would be used for cross-referencing purposes. The first registries I will discuss are those intended to improve the compliance and accuracy of hour credits. It would be necessary to obtain information about the employers and managers that would confer hour credits. The management structures that companies have would be required in order to check for anomalies and to undertake audits and investigations, though it should also be possible to infer this structure from the hour credits that are conferred once the system is up and running. During the overlapping period it would be necessary to assess and train managers in order to ensure that those who will be conferring hour credits are able to do so when the system comes into effect. It would also be necessary to vet them all in order to assess their suitability for such a role, for example if they have been convicted of fraud in the past.

I also suggested registries as a means to combat the potential for income fraud if hourly averaging is combined with a move to comprehensive income taxation. I suggested the introduction of asset registers as a means to track transfers of resources and reduce the scope for income fraud. As a means to this end it would be necessary to specify a particular day on which everyone would have to provide a full inventory of their qualifying items of property. This need not be the same day as that on which hourly averaging or a comprehensive income tax base is introduced—it could happen far in advance. From this day forward any exchange of property would have to be recorded on the relevant registry in order to be legally binding. The value of these exchanges would be automatically shared with the tax authorities from that point forward with tax applied as appropriate.

These new institutions would come into place on particular days as specified by the government introducing the system. However, this does not imply that only information gathered after these appointed days would be utilised in lifetime taxation. In the following section I will discuss the options for taking account of information from *before* the introduction of the system in order to calculate the lifetime taxation of citizens.

Past information

The final issue I will discuss regarding the transition to the CLIPH-rate tax is the utilisation of information on individuals from before the inauguration of the system. The system performs lifetime calculations and so it is clear how it will deal with those who come of age when the system is active. However, decisions would need to be made regarding individuals who have lived some of their lives under the previous system, and I will set out several options in this section.

One option is to start everyone at zero on the first day of the system. This would be the simplest to administer. However, the downside of this approach is that some people will have built up careers and property portfolios which will be taxed very unfairly if their past work is not taken into account. Another extreme option would be to run two systems simultaneously; one system for those who came of age before the introduction of hourly averaging, with hourly averaging only applicable to those who have come of age after the start of the system. However, this is not an attractive option either. It would be very impractical to run two systems side by side. Furthermore, it would not be fair either, since many people would be better off under the alternative system to the one they are on.

I would suggest instead that those who have lived under the previous system would have an amount of hour credits, gross income, and net income set for them in advance of the start of hourly averaging. For example, a date could be set between one and two years prior to the introduction of the system, at which point people's hourly tax accounts could become partially effective. These dates could be staggered to allow analysis of a proportion of taxpayers each week. The information from this point onwards could be applied to their account even though it will not come fully into effect for another year. I have described this possibility in the previous sections. For now, I wish to emphasise how the initial calculation of the starting position for tax accounts could be determined.

It should be possible to determine rough values for hour credits, gross income, and net income. Hour credits can be guesstimated based upon tax payments, job-seeking support payments, student records, number of children born and raised, and social services records regarding caring provision. Primarily, the investigation teams would rely on tax receipts to indicate how many years and months the taxpayer has had full time employment or a relevant proxy. The taxpayer can then be allocated hour credits roughly corresponding to this time spent in employment, say at a rate of thirty seven hours a week if this is a common weekly working contract. Taxpayers could provide copies of contracts and so on if these show that they have worked longer hours, which could lead to an increase in the number of past hour credits they are accredited.

It is more difficult to accurately determine the comprehensive income that individuals have received in their lifetime. However, again a rough proxy will do. The tax information will provide some information as to the income that individuals have received. In addition to this, financial records will indicate any further windfalls that taxpayers have received. If the authorities have access to information on the inheritance received from those who have died this could also be used to populate the fledgling accounts. A team of investigators could scour this information and apply income to recipients accordingly. Finally, the information from asset registers would also be useful to determine income. This is because those who have assets which cost—or are worth—more than the lifetime income that has been calculated for them must have received further income in order to have obtained the items. It would be harder to determine whether people have received gifts that have not left any trace, such as items that have been consumed. However, the information determined using the above means would form a good starting place for tax accounts.

It may seem that we can apply the rough information described above along with the information about the amount of taxes paid by the individual in order to determine the starting values of their account. However, things are not so simple. It is not very likely that the tax paid by the individual would be that which would have been due if they had lived under the CLIPH-rate tax. Therefore when the system starts, taxpayers would either receive a large windfall or face a huge deficit on their account. The accounts should therefore start in a position at which taxpayers are counterfactually assumed to have paid—at least roughly—the correct amount of taxation. The authorities would therefore have to set gross income, net income, and hour credit levels such that they represent the likely past situation of the taxpayer. This could be done by calculating the hourly average that the individual would have paid based on the information available and then adjusting the lifetime gross and net income values in order to ensure that the taxpayer starts their account as if they had paid the correct amount of taxation up until that point.

Conclusion

The purpose of this chapter has been to anticipate concerns regarding the practicalities of introducing the CLIPH-rate tax system when it is so different from pre-existing systems. I first considered the issue of international incompatibility, which could undermine the attempt of any state to introduce the system. This would be a problem due to the potential for tax evasion, avoidance, and competition facilitated by non-compliant states. In response to this I described several international ecosystems in which a state or group of states could introduce the CLIPH-rate tax. The ideal version is one in which states would agree to enforce the same tax base and to share tax revenues from international citizens. This system would divert additional resources from these individuals to those states which would tax the highest, providing a counter-incentive which would arrest the race-to-the-bottom in tax rates.

In the second half of the chapter I discussed the practicalities of the transition from an annual taxation system to a lifetime hourly one. I explained the different periods of the process and what would need to happen in each. I explained the institutions that would need to be created and the pre-existing institutions which would need to be altered. I then explained how the system could be set up in such a way that it can utilise past information and create artificial lifetime averaging accounts for taxpayers who were previously taxed on an annual rather than lifetime basis.

CONCLUSION

Reason for optimism?

In this book I have explained a new form of tax calculation, which I refer to as *hourly averaging*. Allied to this, in chapter four I proposed a new form of tax base, which I have referred to as *comprehensive acquired income*. Together, these two proposals form the CLIPH-rate tax, which stands for *Comprehensive Lifetime Income Per-hour-rate*. When explaining these proposals I indicated why hourly averaging would be a better tax system, particularly in chapter three. I have also offered some further information about the nature of the system and how it could be implemented. In chapters six to eight I discussed some worries that may cause some to question the viability of the proposal, and I will end this book by discussing reasons to be pessimistic or optimistic about the proposals.

With any radical proposal such as that presented in this work it is sensible to proceed with caution. I have given many reasons to be optimistic about the potential benefits of hourly averaging and suggested ways to minimise the downsides of the proposal. On balance, the case seems to me to be obvious; creating a much fairer economic system without a significant loss of economic productivity. Nevertheless, more research would need to be done in order to have greater confidence that the costs of the system would not be greater than I have anticipated, nor its economic consequences more detrimental. To undertake further research before implementing a new system is a sensible idea. However, many people will hide behind this sensible position as a means to postpone the introduction of any major reform.

In any society there will be small minded and ignorant reactionaries who will tend to oppose any reform or change in society, even if they—along with many others—stand to benefit from the change. Other people may hold genuine, though I would claim mistaken, beliefs about justice which would not be compatible with the introduction of the CLIPH-rate tax. These groups would oppose the proposal, and would need to be won over if they were numerous enough to block the introduction of the system.

However, a third group—the elite—will try to fuel these groups against the CLIPH-rate tax, just as they do against many other proposals aimed at creating a fairer and more equal society. Most societies in history have been organised largely for the benefit of a small elite group, and this group will always fight very hard to hold on to power.[110] Those who benefit from the current tax system, or lack of one in some respects, will put large resources into turning people against a proposal such as this.[111] We have seen this happen with many issues, most recently attempts to respond to anthropocentric climate change. As Frederick Douglass once said regarding the emancipation of black people in the USA, 'Power concedes nothing without a demand. It never did and it never will.'[112] Supporters of the CLIPH-rate tax could have a long and frustrating fight for justice, but if all those who would benefit from the system were to mobilise then they would be unstoppable.

I have tried to anticipate some of the excuses that might be made against hourly averaging in this book. I imagine that those opposed to the CLIPH-rate tax would claim—among other things—that the system proposed is as unrealistic as more utopian left-wing proposals, or that it would lead to a totalitarian state. Neither of these claims would be true. Hourly averaging does not require great technological advances or fundamental changes in human nature and ability to coordinate with one another. It would largely work in the same way as other capitalist economic systems. As I discussed in chapter six, totalitarianism could result from many possible changes, and it need not arise due the CLIPH-rate tax. Indeed, the only reliable guard against totalitarianism is a strong rule of law supported by a well informed and active citizenry. As long as the information gathered on citizens, and the anti-fraud investigators, are kept separate from other investigative branches totalitarianism will not arise.

The road to the CLIPH-rate tax would be a long and difficult one. Nevertheless, I will end with some reasons for optimism. I have shown that there are reasons to think that hourly averaging would be beneficial to workers without damaging overall economic productivity and efficiency. I have also shown that it would create a much fairer economic system. This is because the less economically fortune would obtain more resources from their work and those with great economic fortune can be taxed at a higher rate without the usual economic disincentives of doing so. We humans collectively make our society and our politics; if a sufficient number of people generate the political will to introduce hourly averaging, then it will happen.

APPENDIX: EQUATIONS

For the benefit of the mathematically minded, I have expressed the hourly averaging calculation in the following equations. I use the following symbols:

c = hour-credits

g = gross lifetime income

h = gross hourly average income

n = net lifetime income

γ = net hourly average income

β = past net income received

ω = current net income due

t = lifetime tax liability

σ = hourly average tax

ρ = past tax paid

θ = current tax liability

r = Tax-rate, which is expressed decimally. This would have a range of $-\infty$ to ∞, with zero representing no tax and 'one' indicating a one hundred percent tax-rate (though this is never reached or exceeded, as shown in the restrictions below).

I will begin by presenting the stages of the *present or current tax liability calculation*, namely the tax which our taxpayer owes. This is calculated with the hour-credits and gross income of the taxpayer in question, along with the present tax-rates.

Step 1: Calculate gross hourly average income

$$g \div c = h$$

Step 2: Apply the tax-rate (r) to gross average income to calculate the taxpayer's hourly tax level (σ)

$$h \times r = \sigma$$

Step 3: Re-multiply by hour-credits to get total lifetime tax

$$\sigma \times c = t$$

Step 4: Deduct past lifetime tax payments (ρ) to get present tax liability

$$t - \rho = \theta$$

It is possible to calculate *net income due to the individual* from h calculated in step 1 above.

Step 2*: Apply the tax-rate to this average to calculate net hourly income

$$h \times (1 - r) = \gamma$$

Step 3*: Re-multiply by hour-credits to get net lifetime income

$$\gamma \times c = n$$

Step 4*: Deduct past lifetime income received (β) to get current net income due

$$n - \beta = \omega$$

Remember that gross income equals tax plus net income

$$g = n + t$$

This means that from it is possible to cross between one approach at the other at step 3 or 3*.

From step 3 it is possible to reach step 4*

$$g - t - \beta = \omega$$

From 3* it is possible to calculate 4

$$g - n - \rho = \theta$$

That explains the calculation of current liability. I will now present the lifetime equations. The expression for lifetime tax is

$$t = [(\frac{g}{c}) r] c = g - n$$

The expression of lifetime net income is

$$n = (\frac{g}{c}) c (1 - r) = g - t$$

The current-liability equations can be expressed as follows:

$$\omega = [(\frac{g}{c}) (1 - r)] c - \beta$$

$$\theta = [(\frac{g}{c}) r] c - \rho$$

This is subject to the following constraints, the reasoning behind which is found in section 7.8:

A higher hourly average () will result in a higher tax-rate (r).

$$(\frac{\delta r}{\delta \sigma}) > 0$$

An increase in gross income (g) must also always result in an increase in current net income due (ω), which limits the progressivity of the tax. Put differently, the tax-rate will never reach 100%.

$$-\infty < r < 1$$

ENDNOTES

1   Prominent views that would disagree with this point would be libertarian and conservative views. I will not worry about conservatism since it is more of an attitude than a theory. For the preeminent statement of philosophical libertarianism see Robert Nozick, *Anarchy, State, and Utopia* (Oxford: Blackwell, 1974). I do not have much time for libertarianism, and point readers in particular to the following criticisms of the view: G.A. Cohen, Self-Ownership, Freedom, and Equality (Cambridge: Cambridge University Press, 1995) at Ch 10, Samuel Freeman, 'Illiberal Libertarians: Why Libertarianism Is Not a Liberal View', Philosophy & Public Affairs, 30/2 (2001), 105-51, Dworkin, Sovereign Virtue at 110-3, Ronald Dworkin, 'Comment on Narveson: In Defense of Equality', Social Philosophy and Policy, 1/01 (1983), 24-40. For a discussion of the way that libertarian assumptions have invaded debates on taxation see Liam Murphy and Thomas Nagel, *The Myth of Ownership: Taxes and Justice* (Oxford: OUP, 2002).

Despite my wariness regarding libertarianism, I would point out that the tax proposals made here could be compatible with self-ownership-rights-based (i.e. libertarian) views, since these rights can be developed in various ways, for examples see John Philip Christman, *The Myth of Property: Toward an Egalitarian Theory of Ownership* (New York: Oxford University Press, 1994) ix, 219 p, Michael Otsuka, Libertarianism without Inequality (Oxford: Clarendon, 2003).

2   My thought here is that—assuming the acquired comprehensive income tax base were introduced—all financial transfers made into the account of an individual would have tax withheld. Exceptions could be introduced automatically for transfers from other accounts from the same individual. Other non-taxable transfers—such as refunds or payments perks—could be allowed through automatically if pre-approved, or could be recouped through subsequent transfers. It would not matter how much tax was charged on each particular transfer, as long as the tax withheld was accurate at that point in time—a particular transfer could be taxed at 100% or a negative rate through an additional payment from the tax authority.

3   This is the subject of my doctoral thesis; Douglas Bamford, 'Egalitarian Taxation: equality of resources, market luck, and leisure', (University of Warwick, 2013).

4   Ronald Dworkin, 'What Is Equality? Part 2: Equality of Resources', *Philosophy & Public Affairs*, 10/4 (1981), 283-345, reprinted in Ronald Dworkin, *Sovereign Virtue* (Cambridge, Mass: Harvard University Press, 2000) at ch 2, and developed in

ch 9, Dworkin has described his approach more recently in Ronald Dworkin, *Is Democracy Possible Here?* (Princeton, N.J.: Princeton University Press, 2006) at Ch 4, Ronald Dworkin, *Justice for Hedgehogs* (Cambridge, Mass.: Belknap Press of Harvard University Press, 2011) at Ch 16. Other developments of his views on taxation policy can be found in Matthew Clayton, 'Equal Inheritance: An Anti-Perfectionist View', in John Cunliffe and Guido Erreygers (eds.), *Inherited Wealth, Justice and Equality* (London: Routledge, 2012), 98-118, Bamford, 'Egalitarian Taxation',

5   The closest view to Dworkin's is probably the derivative view known as "luck egalitarianism," for an example of which see Eric Rakowski, *Equal Justice* (Oxford: Clarendon Press, 1991). A more recent, and relatively attractive, responsibility-sensitive form of egalitarianism has been presented by Marc Fleurbaey, *Fairness, Responsibility and Welfare* (Oxford: OUP, 2008). Many other distributive views will also find the CLIPH-rate tax attractive. It should be attractive to liberal egalitarians, the most prominent of which is Rawls, whose difference principle suggests that the rules of society should be constituted such that the least well off get as much possible; John Rawls, *A Theory of Justice: Revised Edition* (Oxford: Oxford University Press, 1999) at 47. The proposals fit particularly well with a more left-wing liberal egalitarian view recently expounded by Stuart White, *The Civic Minimum : On the Rights and Obligations of Economic Citizenship* (Oxford: Oxford University Press, 2003).

As well as egalitarian views, I think that the proposal here is compatible with outcome-focused views such as utilitarianism, and—even more clearly—prioritarianism. The former is the view that utility should be maximised, associated with Jeremy Bentham, *Selected Writings on Utilitarianism* (Ware, Herts.: Wordsworth, 2000). The tax system proposed here fits this ideal if we make two plausible assumptions; there is no way to determine which people are "utility-monsters" who will be the most efficient converters of resources into utility, and second that resources have a broadly diminishing marginal utility—so a millionaire gets less pleasure from a dollar than a pauper does. Prioritarianism holds that utility should be enlarged while giving preference to the utility of those with the least utility, see Derek Parfit, 'Equality or Priority?', in Matthew Clayton and Andrew Williams (eds.), *The Ideal of Equality* (Basingstoke: MacMillan, 2000), 81-125.

6   Adam Smith, *An Inquiry into the Nature and Causes of the Wealth of Nations* (New York: P F Collier and Son, 1909 [1784]) at 498-501.

7   Recent developments in taxation policies seem to result in greater taxation on those with average fortune, without taxing the most fortunate any more. This is partly driven by libertarian (or neo-liberal) ideology, and partly by the existence of tax havens as a means for the most fortunate to hide their wealth from taxation.

8   The definition of progressive taxation is that the average tax rate rises as the tax-base rises, which can also be explained as the marginal rate of tax being higher than the average rate of tax at any given point on the tax-base, James A. Mirrlees and IFS, *Tax by Design: The Mirrlees Review* (Oxford: Oxford University Press, 2011) at 24.

9   This should, of course, be focussed upon the worst-off in the world. It is a moral
    duty for societies, but owed particularly by societies who restrict entry—legiti-
    mately—to their labour markets.

10 I will discuss this point again on page 64-5.

11 Of course, while stability is a good feature, this should not be interpreted in an
    overly conservative manner. It does not mean that we should never make any
    changes for fear of inconveniencing taxpayers. Rather, it is an imperative to move
    to a superior system if one is available. However, one criterion by which to test the
    superiority of a proposed system is that it will be stable and convenient.

12 An exception here is where taxes are designed to protect the environment or im-
    prove society for future generations instead of unsustainable short-term growth.
    My focus in this book is on personal taxation, and I am ignoring environmental
    and Pigovian (more commonly known as "sin") taxes in this work.

13 Emmanuel Saez, 'Optimal Income Transfer Programs: Intensive Versus Extensive
    Labor Supply Responses', *The Quarterly Journal of Economics*, 117/3 (2002), 1039-
    73, Edmund S. Phelps, *Rewarding Work : How to Restore Participation and Self-
    Support to Free Enterprise* (Cambridge, Mass.: Harvard University Press, 1997),
    Guy Laroque, 'Income Maintenance and Labor Force Participation', *Economet-
    rica*, 73/2 (2005), 341-76, Mike Brewer, Emmanuel Saez, and Andrew Shephard,
    'Means-Testing and Tax Rates on Earnings', in Stuart Adam et al. (eds.), *Dimen-
    sions of Tax Design: The Mirrlees Review* (Oxford: Oxford University Press, 2010),
    Philippe Choné and Guy Laroque, 'Optimal Incentives for Labor Force Participa-
    tion', *Journal of Public Economics*, 89/2-3 (2005), 395-425.

14 Thorstein Veblen, *The Theory of the Leisure Class* (New York: Modern Library,
    2001 [1899]). Taxing windfalls of this kind may therefore increase the amount of
    work done by some people.

15 There is no reason why averaging could not be applied to other types of tax calcu-
    lation, such as a consumption tax. I will discuss the tax base in chapter five.

16 For example in Wisconsin and Australia in the 1920s and 30s, and as part of US
    federal income tax from the 1960s to 80s. See William Vickrey, *Agenda for Progres-
    sive Taxation (with a New Introduction)* (Clifton N.J.: Augustus M. Kelley, 1972)
    at 105-6, William Vickrey, *Public Economics: Selected Papers by William Vickrey*
    (Cambridge: Cambridge University Press, 1994) at 169-72. The US federal system
    changes were introduced in the Internal Revenue Code §§ 1301-1305 (1964), and
    discussed in Richard Schmalbeck, 'Income Averaging after Twenty Years: A Failed
    Experiment in Horizontal Equity', *Duke Law Journal*, 3 (1984), 509-80. In addi-
    tion to moving averages like this one, averaging has been allowed for particular
    professions, including authors and inventors in the UK (thanks to Andy Reeve for
    pointing this out to me).

17 It is possible to apply lifetime averaging without any kind of averaging, of course.
    Such a proposal was made by Herwig J. Schlunk, 'A Lifetime Income Tax', *Virginia
    Tax Review*, 25/4 (2006), 939-76. The sole advantage of this proposal seems to be
    that it makes it easier for people to shift resources from later to earlier stages in
    their adult lives without having to pay the risk premium on private borrowing.

However, if this is a good idea, it is possible to enable such inter-personal transfers in a much more targeted manner through the provision of low-interest government loans for students and young parents, or the provision of subsidised childcare.

18 Moving averages are problematic because the averaging period contains different income each time, yet income from a particular period appears in several separate averaging calculations. The moving average calculation, however, does not account for all of these past tax payments based partially on the same income, with arbitrary and unfair results. Moving averages can result in high taxes when people have a lower income and are less able to pay. Furthermore, it can reduce taxes for some people with high overall income.

19 Vickrey's original article on averaging was published as William Vickrey, 'Averaging of Income for Income-Tax Purposes', *Journal of Political Economy*, 47/3 (1939), 379-97. This was reprinted in Vickrey, *Public Economics: Selected Papers by William Vickrey* at ch 5. In 1947 he published a book length exposition of the proposal for cumulative averaging, later reissued as Vickrey, *Agenda for Progressive Taxation*.

20 Though I note that many such self-employed workers have scope to smooth out their income such that it is received in less variable portions. Artists and musicians can receive "advance payment" from publishers. Those who have companies can use their company status to defer payments from their company accounts to themselves in order to pay themselves during fallow and re-training periods.

21 Tax averaging also has the advantage that it smooths the taxpayer's income out over time, as mentioned at 58.

22 I have been asked why hours are preferable to minutes or seconds, for example by Liam Shields. There is no philosophical reason to prefer hours, only practical ones. I have chosen hours as they are sufficiently accurate and accounting for hours would be less demanding for workers and employers. Most people are employed on contracts with specified hours. If hours were felt to be too restrictive then I would suggest it would be better to introduce half-hour credits and quarter-hour credits rather than switch to minutes.

23 Employers would need to be registered for fraud compliance reasons. Conferring hour credits will reduce tax revenues, as well as effecting greater transfers to the recipients through lower tax rates. Therefore fraud of this kind would be doubly expensive to the government and the rest of society. I will discuss hour credits in greater detail in chapter two, and fraud in chapter seven.

24 Clearly there would need to be strong anti-fraud measures in order to ensure that employers and employees do not collude to overstate the amount of hours worked. These would include cross-referencing employment advertisements, job offers, and contracts and the enforcement of serious penalties for firms and managers who are found guilty of hour credit fraud.

25 Though there may be scope to allow deferred tax payments for those who have a sudden decrease in net income.

26 The UK government is introducing "Real-Time" taxation calculations at the time of writing (Summer 2013). This system replaces the old approach of applying a tax code to each taxpayer, which is often wrong, with a system that informs employers

how much tax to withhold on each transaction. I have imagined a similar system being utilised to calculation lifetime hourly averaging.

27 Though there may be scope to allow those who have a sudden decrease in net income to defer their tax payments.

28 The calculation could just as well be undertaken on the basis of *tax paid* in the past in order to calculate *tax due* in the latest period. This is because gross income equals net income plus tax.

29 I will discuss this issue further in chapter seven on hour credit fraud.

30 For the precise definition of progressive taxation see endnote 8.

31 I discuss this issue in more detail on page 60.

32 Those who have worked for extremely large fortunes—or potential fortunes where they have not cashed them in—have usually obtained those amounts by finding ways to obtain rents. Bill Gates, Amancio Ortega, Warren Buffet, and Carlos Slim (the four richest people in the world in 2013, according to Forbes) have been very successful at finding investments which will earn larger rents than others. Gates, for example, has made much of his fortune through a monopolistic position in the computer software market. I do not think that taxing these individuals at a higher rate would not have had a significant effect on their productivity. It should be noted that these individuals would have been able to build up their fortunes without taxation given the tax base that I advocate in chapter four. The individuals named would not have been taxed at the extremely high rates since they have not yet "cashed in" most of their investments and consumed them or transferred them for their personal use.

33 I present these as graphs rather than stepped "bands" because the bands actually imply a graph anyway. In addition, it is highly advisable to have very smooth rate-changes, for reasons I explained on page 7, see also page 66-8.

34 That is, that the tax rate is progressive throughout.

35 That is, the graph should never slope back over itself, which would create the impossible situation of two tax rates applying to a particular income. This would also violate the following constraints.

36 These last two points ensure that the marginal rate on increasing income never reaches 100%. The graph, essentially, must always rise or be level as income increases. The gradient of the slope must be less than infinity (or less than 90 degrees from the horizontal line) and be positive or zero (or no less than 0 degrees). I express these constraints mathematically in the appendix. It is important to remember that marginal tax rates do not work in the same way with hourly-averaging as with any other tax system. This is because the decision to work an additional hour will have a *reducing* effect on the person's lifetime tax rate. With other systems the individual's marginal tax rate simply applies on their next hour (or however long) worked, and so the headline rate is much more important.

37 Except those who receive a large windfall early in life, who may jump from one extreme of the graph to the other.

38 Or whatever unit of time they contract to.

39   One interesting question, which would need to be resolved before the introduc-
     tion of the system, is how to account for time that workers spend away on holiday.
     For example, should workers obtain hour credits for bank holidays that they do
     not work? Furthermore, should workers be able to receive hour credits for time
     spent on annual leave? I will leave these questions open at this stage, as it would
     be up to those implementing the system to decide how inclusive to be with these
     matters. However, I will précis some of the possible issues in the paragraph below.

     It seems sensible to allow firms to pay hour credits for time spent on leave as
     detailed in the employment contract between employer and employee. However,
     this leads to a worry that this will create a loophole through which employers can
     pay their employees through hour credits (which are free for them) instead of
     money. If this were proven to be possible, then it might be necessary to impose a
     maximum number of hour credits that workers could receive for time spent on
     leave. This could be calculated as a proportion of hour credits earned from work-
     ing on the job, for example that after every twelve hour credits earned the worker
     should receive an entitlement to one hour credit of holiday, to be taken at some
     point in the same annual period. As long as the holiday and regular hour credits
     were in the correct proportion by the end of the year this would be acceptable.
     This also opens the possibility that there could be exceptions to this rule for some
     jobs which are very unpopular in order to increase the numbers undertaking
     them. This could apply to jobs that are very intense and which workers will only
     undertake if they can obtain both a large income and a large amount of vacation.

40   Though of course this virtual information should be backed-up on to more per-
     manent media at regular intervals.

41   Schemes of government employment have been utilised in the past, for example
     in the USA during the 1930s depression. Phillip Harvey advocates a similar Em-
     ployment Assistance Programme, though funded directly rather than through
     the tax system: Philip Harvey, *Securing the Right to Employment: Social Welfare
     Policy and the Unemployed in the United States* (Princeton, NJ: Princeton Univer-
     sity Press, 1989) at 21-78, Philip Harvey, 'Funding a Job Guarantee', *International
     Journal of Environment, Workplace and Employment*, 2/1 (2006), 114-32, Philip
     Harvey, 'Securing the Right to Work at the State or Local Level with a Direct Job
     Creation Program', *Big Ideas for Jobs Initiative* <http://www.bigideasforjobs.org/
     wp-content/uploads/2011/09/Harvey-Full-Report-2-PDF.pdf>

42   Hyman Minsky described a similar scheme, though designed with the slightly dif-
     ferent aim of pushing up wages for low-skilled workers; Hyman Minsky, 'The Role
     of Employment Policy', in Margaret Gordon (ed.), Poverty in America (San Fran-
     cisco: Chandler Publishing Company, 1965), 175-200. Minsky therefore proposes
     interventions that would seek to 'make labor more homogenous and that generate
     demand for the unemployed, relatively low wage workers.' He also suggests that
     government should assist people in relocating from low to high employment areas
     and should interfere in the market to encourage high skilled jobs to be broken
     down into many low skilled ones in order to create more employment; Minsky,
     'The Role of Employment Policy', at 194-5.

43 Richard Layard, *Happiness : Lessons from a New Science* (New York: Penguin Press, 2005) at 67. For some panel-data based evidence on the effects of unemployment see; Liliana Winkelmann and Rainer Winkelmann, 'Why Are the Unemployed So Unhappy? Evidence from Panel Data', *Economica*, 65/257 (1998), 1-15, Peter Warr, Paul Jackson, and Michael Banks, 'Unemployment and Mental Health: Some British Studies', *Journal of Social Issues*, 44/4 (1988), 47-68, Andrew Clark, Yannis Georgellis, and Peter Sanfey, 'Scarring: The Psychological Impact of Past Unemployment', *Economica*, 68/270 (2001), 221-41.

44 The value of the care undertaken in the UK has been estimated at a massive £119bn, which is greater than the budget of the National Health Service, in Lisa Buckner and Sue Yeandle, 'Valuing Carers: Calculating the Value of Carers' Support', (Carers UK, 2011). The estimate may be high, and the research was undertaken on behalf of a group seeking further support for carers. However, the point remains that carers provide a great service to society as well as those they assist.

45 Except perhaps women who are raped and who feel unable to go through with an abortion.

46 Madeline Bunting, *Willing Slaves: How the Overwork Culture Is Ruling Our Lives* (Harper Perennial, 2004).

47 This is recognised in European Union law through the *working time directive* (Directive 2003/88/EC), which states that employers cannot force workers to work more than 48 hours a week. An eye-opening description of examples of overly long hours and the effects thereof is provided by Karl Marx, *Capital: A Critique of Political Economy* (London: Penguin, 1990 [1867]) at ch 10, secs 3-4.

48 This would mean the payee would receive no net income until they had paid off this debt. In some cases it will not be acceptable to leave someone in a position where they would have to live without any income—if they do not have any assets to sell they may have no alternative but to commit further crimes in order to survive—in which case, those without assets could perhaps receive a small loan each month which would also be added to their future liabilities. Perhaps it might be necessary to limit the economic freedom of those who continually rack-up debts without showing any desire to alter their behaviour, perhaps by providing them with the food and shelter of their choice, plus a small amount for discretionary spending, within a set budget in exchange for work performed until their debts were paid off.

49 A legitimate society is one in which the members of the society have no cause to overthrow the political system. While it may not be perfect, it attempts to treat its citizens in an equal fashion. A fully just society would do a good job of showing equal concern for all its members. See Dworkin, *Justice for Hedgehogs* at 321-2.

50 Vickrey, 'Averaging of Income for Income-Tax Purposes', at 379.

51 For this reason, there is provision for authors to effectively average out their income in the UK. In some cases also those with fluctuating incomes can find ways to smooth their incomes—such as advance payments for authors and deferred dividends for small business owners.

52 If job sharing is not felt to adequately resolve this issue then a further option is to provide special dispensation to those who undertake unpopular forms of work. This could be described as hour credit worthy "recovery time" included as part of the specified jobs.

53 The most well-known philosophical argument for a basic income is found in Philippe Van Parijs, *Real Freedom for All : What (If Anything) Can Justify Capitalism?* (Oxford: Clarendon Press, 1995).

54 See the chapters reprinted in John Cunliffe and Guido Erreygers, *The Origins of Universal Grants: An Anthology of Historical Writings on Basic Capital and Basic Income* (Basingstoke, Hampshire: Palgrave Macmillan, 2004) at Part 1.

55 I.e. a grant to all members of the demos (Greek word for 'population').

56 Bruce A. Ackerman and Anne Alstott, *The Stakeholder Society* (New Haven, Conn.: Yale University Press, 1999) at Ch 1.

57 As in, a minimum income that all people will receive irrespective of anything other than citizenship.

58 Milton Friedman, *Capitalism and Freedom* (Chicago: University of Chicago Press, 1962) at 191-2.

59 I will describe these schemes in broad terms since they change often. Indeed, the WTC is scheduled to be replaced in the near future by the "Universal Credit," which combines unemployment benefit and earning subsidy payments into one system, as is done by this hourly averaging proposal. However, without hourly averaging this scheme will face the same difficulties and expense as its predecessor scheme.

60 The weekly hour requirement for WTC assistance was increased from eighteen hours to twenty-four on the 6th of April 2012.

61 Phelps, *Rewarding Work.*

62 On the basis that employers will not pay workers more than their labour productivity allows, George J. Stigler, 'The Economics of Minimum Wage Legislation', *The American Economic Review*, 36/3 (1946), 358-65. Some have questioned whether the real economy works as this textbook example shows, most notably David E. Card and Alan B. Krueger, *Myth and Measurement : The New Economics of the Minimum Wage* (Princeton, N.J.: Princeton University Press, 1995).

63 Endowment taxation is particularly popular with utilitarians, and economists have generally followed their forbears in this regard; For a review article see Lawrence Zelenak, 'Taxing Endowment', *Duke Law Journal*, 55/6 (2006), 1145-82. James Mirrlees took endowment taxation to be the ideal tax from which he developed his famous optimal taxation theory; James A. Mirrlees, 'An Exploration in the Theory of Optimum Income Taxation', *The Review of Economic Studies*, 38/2 (1971), 175-208. For a recent critique of Mirrlees' economistic approach on the basis of its endowment-based underpinnings see Linda Sugin, 'A Philosophical Objection to the Optimal Tax Model', *Tax Law Review*, 64 (2011), 229-81.

64 See Dworkin's discussion of a similar endowment-based proposal in his hypothetical island example; Dworkin, *Sovereign Virtue* at 90-1. As well as the problem of enslaving the talented, endowment taxation has the further issue that it is very

difficult to determine people's endowments in the first place—people will have both the incentive and the means to hide their endowments. This point has been mentioned in John Rawls, *Justice as Fairness: A Restatement* (Cambridge, Mass.: Harvard University Press, 2001) at 157-8, Liam Murphy and Thomas Nagel, *The Myth of Ownership: Taxes and Justice*, (Oxford: OUP, 2002) at 122, Stuart White, 'The Egalitarian Earnings Subsidy Scheme', *British Journal of Political Science*, 29/4 (1999), 601-22 at 603, Dworkin, Sovereign Virtue at 100.

65 Problems with the idea of distributing in accordance with welfare are presented in Dworkin, *Sovereign Virtue* at ch 1, Amartya Sen, 'Utilitarianism and Welfarism', *The Journal of Philosophy*, 76/9 (1979), 463-89. One argument against welfarism can be expressed in terms of a continuity test, whereby people cannot claim in good faith that they are unfairly treated with regard to their welfare unless they were to accept that they should live their lives solely with regard to that kind of welfare; see Andrew Williams, 'Equality for the Ambitious', *Philosophical Quarterly*, 52 (2002), 377-89 at 387-9.

66 See page 28.

67 See page 7 and endnote 13.

68 In the previous section I acknowledged that hourly averaging may cause price increases on some items. This would occur if there are jobs that workers will only undertake if they earn many times the average net wage. The gross income required to achieve such a premium would rise hugely with progressive hourly averaging, with the cost passed on to consumers. If it is not possible to pass on the cost of this, presumably by sharing it among numerous consumers, then the work would not be undertaken. I would not think that there would not be many cases of this sort, whereas there would be numerous cases in which valuable work may be undertaken by workers paid below an acceptable minimum income for that society.

69 See endnote 13.

70 William F. Mitchell, 'The Buffer Stock Employment Model and the Nairu: The Path to Full Employment', *Journal of Economic Issues*, 32/2 (1998), 547-55. Mitchell is one of a number of post-Keynesian economists who support job creation schemes for economic reasons. See also R. Wray, *Understanding Modern Money: The Key to Full Employment and Price Stability* (Cheltenham, UK: Edward Elgar, 1998), W.B. Mosler, 'Full Employment and Price Stability', *Journal of Post Keynesian Economics,* 20/2 (1998), 167-82, William Mitchell and Joan Muysken, *Full Employment Abandoned: Shifting Sands and Policy Failures* (Cheltenham: Edward Elgar, 2008).

71 I will discuss such a mandatory pension scheme again on page 110.

72 This is known as "stamp duty" in the UK, as the authorities have to "stamp" their approval on the transfer of land ownership

73 That is, to introduce a lifetime accession tax—either cumulative or averaged—on gifts and windfalls. For accession tax proposals see Harry J Rudick, 'A Proposal for an Accessions Tax', *Tax Law Review*, 1/1 (1945), 25-44, William D. Andrews, 'The Accessions Tax Proposal', *Tax Law Review*, 22 (1966), 589-634, Cedric Thomas Sandford et al., *An Accessions Tax : A Study of the Desirability and Feasibiliy of Re-*

placing the United Kingdom Estate Duty by a Cumulative Tax on Recipients of Gifts and Inheritances (London: Institute for Fiscal Studies, 1973), Edward C. Jr. Halbach, 'An Accessions Tax', *Real Property Probate & Trust Journal*, 23 (1988), 211-27.

74   Perhaps more accurate than taxpayer would be "taxable unit," given that I will suggest in the following section that it should possible for couples to officially combine their tax accounts if they combine their other economic affairs.

75   It is therefore referred to as "S-H-S" in Richard Goode, 'The Economic Definition of Income', in Joseph A. Pechman (ed.), *Comprehensive Income Taxation* (Washington D.C.: Brookings Institute, 1977), 1-30. Goode adds Schanz to the Haig-Simons moniker as he suggested similar several decades prior to the other two; Georg Von Schanz, 'Der Einkommensbegriff Und Die Einkommensteuergesetze', *Finanzarchiv*, 13 (1896), 1–87, Robert M. Haig, 'The Concept of Income— Economic and Legal Aspects', in Richard A. Musgrave and Carl S. Shoup (eds.), *Readings in the Economics of Taxation* (Homewood, Ill.: Irwin, for the American Economic Association, 1959), Henry Calvert Simons, *Personal Income Taxation: The Definition of Income as a Problem of Fiscal Policy* (Chicago, Ill.: University of Chicago Press, 1938). My exposition is based upon Simons.

76   For a sample of writing in favour of consumption taxation see Nicholas Kaldor, *An Expenditure Tax* (London: Allen & Unwin, 1955), William D. Andrews, 'A Consumption-Type or Cash Flow Personal Income Tax', *Harvard Law Review*, 87/6 (1974), 1113-88, Laurence Seidman, *The USA Tax: A Progressive Consumption Tax* (Cambridge, Mass.: MIT Press, 1997), Edward J. McCaffery, *Fair Not Flat: How to Make the Tax System Better and Simpler* (Chicago: Chicago University Press, 2002).

Support for consumption taxation has been traced back to Thomas Hobbes, Leviathan (Harmondsworth, Eng.: Penguin, 1986 [1651]) at 386, see Dudley Jackson, 'Thomas Hobbes' Theory of Taxation', *Political Studies*, 21/2 (1973), 175-82 at 180. However, whether Hobbes really meant what we now consider consumption taxation is controversial. We can be more certain that such prominent thinkers as J.S. Mill and John Rawls have endorsed consumption taxes; John Stuart Mill, *Principles of Political Economy: Books Iv and V* (London: Penguin, 1970) at 164 (Book V, Ch 2, S4), Rawls, *A Theory of Justice: Revised Edition* at 246.

77   This possible tax base is mentioned by Vickrey, *Agenda for Progressive Taxation* at 194-5.

78   I will anticipate a response to my proposals that clever people may come up with after reading this example. They may respond that since a) all labour is a form of exchange of time for money and b) exchanged property would not be subject to tax, therefore income from labour should not count under this definition. However, while the sale of labour is a form of exchange involving property of value, labour is not itself a form of property of the relevant kind. The sale and purchase of labour is a specific and separate type of transaction and its inclusion in the tax base should be considered on its own merits. Therefore, this argument does not undermine the acquired income tax base.

Anyone attracted to the left-libertarian position, described above as a result of a worry that taxation is generally skewed against workers, should note that hourly averaging reduces the taxation on work. This means that the proposals in this book are much more generous to those who obtain their income from working than other tax proposals (except those which would not tax workers at all, though the lack of tax revenue which would render many workers worse off — along with those who cannot work for reasons beyond their control).

79 Though it would not enable the investor to reduce their current tax liability, as the consumption tax would.

80 Tax data on citizens has long been available in Scandinavian countries such as Norway and Sweden, and I see no serious reason to restrict people from finding limited information on persons of known name or address. If the address were given alongside the name then this might be a problem, as it would enable unscrupulous or dangerous people to target well known persons. However, if someone knows of an address or someone's name then it should be possible to find out their tax information.

81 Boris Bittker, 'A "Comprehensive Tax Base" As a Goal of Income Tax Reform', *Harvard Law Review*, 80/5 (1967), 925-85.

82 There may be a scope to allow exceptions to this. For example, if a child has relatives who live in remote and expensive locations then the cost of the travel to visit them might not be counted as part of the usual allowance.

83 For a discussion of this issue, though more from the perspective of the parent, see; Harry Brighouse, 'Egalitarian Liberalism and Justice in Education', *The Political Quarterly*, 73/2 (2002), 181-90 at 184, Adam Swift, *How Not to Be a Hypocrite : School Choice for the Morally Perplexed* (London; New York: Routledge, 2003) at particularly 23-5, Harry Brighouse and Adam Swift, 'Legitimate Parental Partiality', *Philosophy & Public Affairs*, 37/1 (2009), 43-80. I mentioned the idea of *positional goods* in education, as Swift and Brighouse do also. Positional goods are important because no matter how wealthy a society becomes, these goods will only be available to those who have more than others. This means that distributive issues are therefore always highly important. The idea originally came from Fred Hirsch, *Social Limits to Growth* (Cambridge, Mass.: Harvard University Press, 1976).

84 Remember that, as was the case regarding asset registers, taxpayers have an incentive to specify their property at this point, as if the gains they obtain when selling it will be counted against its value at this point in time. If a taxpayer does not register an item of property that they own at this point then when they come to sell it or give it away then *all of its value* would be counted as a gain.

85 Conversely, it might be advisable to provide those with few assets at adulthood with some additional gross funds in their tax account which will compensate them for their relative disadvantage in familial generosity.

86 Governments usually attempt to keep inflation at relatively low levels. Incompetent and crisis-riven governments have printed money, but given that this causes *hyperinflation* it is not considered a sensible policy.

87 Closing tax accounts and creating a new one was Vickrey's proposal to allow merged accounts: Vickrey, *Agenda for Progressive Taxation* at 186-7. See also Vickrey, *Public Economics: Selected Papers by William Vickrey* at 115, 25.

88 Another worry related to this one might be that of "chain marriages." These would be marriages designed to keep large income and hour credits gained in the past in circulation by transferring them through marriage from one person to another. If this was deemed a problem then it might be considered necessary to impose additional rules on those who remarry after the death of a partner. While they may be able to keep the past wealth and hour credits from their deceased spouse until remarriage, the surviving spouse would have to go through the equivalent of the divorce procedure before being able to create a new joint account.

89 This potential "floodgates" problem for time-based lifetime averaging was discussed by both Pechman and Schmalbeck: Joseph A. Pechman, *Federal Tax Policy, Fourth Edition* (Washington D.C.: The Brookings Institution, 1983) at 122, Richard Schmalbeck, 'Income Averaging after Twenty Years: A Failed Experiment in Horizontal Equity', *Duke Law Journal*, 1984/3 (1984), 509-80 at 571. Pechman suggests that averaging is appealing if it is possible to 'avoid including retired persons in the averaging system.' However, it is not that easy to close tax accounts upon retirement, as retirement is not always such a clear-cut thing. Individuals may retire and then later change their minds, leaving an island of retirement surrounded by periods of work. This issue is less problematic with the introduction of hour credits, since people can stop and restart earning them.

90 There is, of course, significant disagreement among economists regarding the appropriateness of government intervention and non-intervention for macroeconomic reasons. I take it as reasonably uncontroversial that markets (or at least a significant proportion of investors) can sometimes become overly exuberant during boom times and overly pessimistic during busts, and that states need to act in some way to counterbalance this.

91 There is no reliable information on the proportion of the wealth in the UK, for example, owned by the wealthiest individuals. The government does not systematically collect these statistics, and in any case many wealthy individuals have hidden their resources away in secrecy jurisdictions (tax havens) in order to avoid or evade taxation. However, even the limited information available from estate taxation indicates that 53% of the wealth was owned by the top 10% of those who died in the period 2008-10 (see http://www.hmrc.gov.uk/statistics/wealth/table13-8.pdf, published as part of http://www.hmrc.gov.uk/statistics/wealth/personal-wealth.pdf).

The true wealth statistics would indicate a much higher proportion of the wealth being held by the top 10% than these statistics indicate. This would be the case since some poorer individuals do not have their wealth assessed upon death, and most wealthy people will have given away much of their wealth prior to death, in order to avoid estate taxation. I therefore think it is safe to conclude that a significant amount of wealth is held by a very small number of individuals, particularly so with regard to productively invested wealth (as opposed to personal wealth such as jewellery and housing).

92 One response to this point would be to highlight that those with significant wealth need not give their wealth to a small number of individuals. One alternative would be for the wealthy to spread out their bequests to a very large number of people

who would each pay a lower amount of tax, with the result that less of the wealth would be taxed. However, in this case the economic concerns still arise, of course, to the extent that the recipients would have money to spend and there would be fewer resources invested throughout the economy.

Another alternative would be for the wealthy to gift their resources to a charity. However, according to the acquired income tax-base this would count as a form of consumption which would be attributed to the individual and therefore taxed at a very high rate. This would also be the result for wealthy individuals after the first generation when they bequeath their resources—these bequests would be constructively realised and counted as gains for the recently deceased individual and be taxed at a high rate.

93 An additional change may arise if it were made compulsory for taxpayers to invest in pension funds, as I discussed on page 110. This would counteract somewhat the tendency for those with low earnings and wealth to have higher short-term spending and lower long-term saving rates than wealthier individuals.

94 Geoffrey Brennan and James M. Buchanan, *The Power to Tax : Analytical Foundations of a Fiscal Constitution* (Cambridge: Cambridge University Press, 1980).

95 Eugene Bardach, 'Moral Suasion and Taxpayer Compliance', Law & Policy, 11/1 (1989), 49-69.

96 Maria Sigala, Carole B. Burgoyne, and Paul Webley, 'Tax Communication and Social Influence: Evidence from a British Sample', *Journal of Community & Applied Social Psychology*, 9/3 (1999), 237-41, Michael Wenzel, 'Misperceptions of Social Norms About Tax Compliance: From Theory to Intervention', *Journal of Economic Psychology*, 26/6 (2005), 862-83, Michael Wenzel, 'An Analysis of Norm Processes in Tax Compliance', *Journal of Economic Psychology*, 25/2 (2004), 213-28, Michael Wenzel, 'The Impact of Outcome Orientation and Justice Concerns on Tax Compliance: The Role of Taxpayers' Identity', *Journal of Applied Psychology*, 87/4 (2002), 629-45. The "slippery slope" framework is a useful way of thinking about tax compliance, see Erich Kirchler, *The Economic Psychology of Tax Behaviour* (Cambridge: Cambridge University Press, 2007), Erich Kirchler, Erik Hoelzl, and Ingrid Wahl, 'Enforced Versus Voluntary Tax Compliance: The "Slippery Slope" Framework', *Journal of Economic Psychology*, 29/2 (2008), 210-25.

97 Michael Wenzel, 'A Letter from the Tax Office: Compliance Effects of Informational and Interpersonal Justice', Social Justice Research, 19/3 (2006), 345-64.

98 John T. Scholz and Mark Lubell, 'Trust and Taxpaying: Testing the Heuristic Approach to Collective Action', *American Journal of Political Science,* 42/2 (1998), 398-417, Wenzel, 'The Impact of Outcome Orientation and Justice Concerns on Tax Compliance: The Role of Taxpayers' Identity', Wenzel, 'An Analysis of Norm Processes in Tax Compliance'.

99 Gary S. Becker, 'Crime and Punishment: An Economic Approach', *Journal of Political Economy*, 76/2 (1968), 169-217, Michael G. Allingham and Agnar Sandmo, 'Income Tax Evasion: A Theoretical Analysis', *Journal of Public Economics*, 1/3–4 (1972), 323-38. These approaches are economic developments of the consequentialist approach to punishment, early advocates of which were Cesare Beccaria, *An Essay on Crimes and Punishments*, trans. Edward D. Ingraham (Philadelphia:

Nicklin and Walker, 1819 (1764)), Jeremy Bentham, *An Introduction to the Principles of Morals and Legislation* (Oxford: Clarendon Press, 1907 [1780]). There are other philosophical approaches to punishment (deontic, retributivist, or liberal), for a summary see Hugo Adam Bedau and Erin Kelly, 'Punishment', *Stanford Encyclopedia of Philosophy* <http://plato.stanford.edu/entries/punishment/>, accessed 2nd August 2013.

100 The idea of using nudging has received a lot of attention recently following the work by Richard H. Thaler and Cass R. Sunstein, *Nudge* (Cornwall: Yale University Press, 2008).

101 Of course the official contract might be signed with a secret understanding that the number of hours will in fact be less. If this agreement is not detected by the authorities when the agreement is made or reported by suspicious colleagues or neighbours, then the fake contract may unravel of its own accord. This is because the existence of the legally binding fake contract renders the secret agreement unstable. The worker knows that their employer could enforce the official contract at any time and get more work from them. The worker therefore has little reason to trust that they will continue to receive illicit hour credits in the long run. They have no recourse to complain if they are asked to work all the hours stated in the contract, and so companies will tend to do this if they think it will be worthwhile.

102 This could be supplemented by school records, online social networks, telephone records, and so on if this was not felt to be too intrusive.

103 Ceyhun Elgin and Oguz Oztunali, 'Shadow Economies All around the World: Model-Based Estimates', <http://www.voxeu.org/article/shadow-economies-around-world-model-based-estimates>. Of course, estimates of the shadow economies are always difficult and somewhat unreliable; Edgar L. Feige and Ivica Urban, 'Measuring Underground (Unobserved, Non-Observed, Unrecorded) Economies in Transition Countries: Can We Trust Gdp?', *Journal of Comparative Economics*, 36/2 (2008), 287-306.

104 Sally Martinez-Vazquez, Jorge Alm, James Wallace, *Taxing the Hard-to-Tax Lessons from Theory and Practice* (Bingley: Emerald Group Publishing Limited, 2010).

105 Nicholas Shaxson and Ellie Mae O'Hagan, 'Mythbusters: "A Competitive Tax System Is a Better Tax System"', *Mythbusters* (London: New Economics Foundation, 2013).

106 Charles M. Tiebout, 'A Pure Theory of Local Expenditures', *Journal of Political Economy*, 64/5 (1956), 416-24.

107 See endnote 1 above.

108 Such a suggestion is made by Peter Dietsch and Thomas Rixen, 'Tax Competition and Global Background Justice', *Journal of Political Philosophy*, (forthcoming). The authors summarise their paper here: http://www.cepweb.org/the-case-for-an-international-tax-organisation/.

109 For a more detailed presentation of the proposal see; Douglas Bamford, 'Comprehensive Lifetime Taxation of International Citizens: A Solution to Tax Avoidance, Tax Competition, and Tax Unfairness', in Jeremy Leaman and Attiya Waris (eds.),

Tax Justice and the Political Economy of Global Capitalism (Oxford: Berghahn Books, 2013).

110 The classical elite theorists are Vilfredo Pareto, Gaetano Mosca, and Robert Michels. Where power is held in a more *plural* basis it may be that there is a coalition of groups who hold illegitimate amounts of power, and these groups together would fight against CLIPH-rate tax. The problem for the spread of the CLIPH-rate tax is that it benefits those who tend to be the least powerful and organised members of society, at the expense of whichever group or groups are currently benefitting from society.

111 The tools of the reactionary have been documented by Albert O. Hirschman, *The Rhetoric of Reaction: Perversity, Futility, Jeopardy* (Cambridge, Mass.: Belknap Press of Harvard University Press, 1991).

112 Frederick Douglass, *Two Speeches* (Rochester, N.Y.: O. P. Dewey, 1857) at 22. This is available online at http://www.libraryweb.org/~digitized/books/Two_Speeches_by_Frederick_Douglass.pdf (accessed 5th June 2013), and the speech can also be found at Frederick Douglass, 'An Address on West India Emancipation', <http://www.lib.rochester.edu/index.cfm?PAGE=4398>.

INDEX

Abuse of power:
    by governments 122-6
    by managers 127-8
Accessions 8, 21-2, 48, 54, 78-9, 189-90 en73
Accretion, see Tax base: Comprehensive income
Acquired Income tax base, see Tax base: acquired income
Additional hour credits:
    For carers 43-4
    For disability 37-8
    For students 41-3
    Maximum, applied to additional hour credits 45
Andrews, William 189 en73
Annual taxation:
    Compared to lifetime taxation 13, 14, 105
    Disadvantages of 14, 53-60
    Switching from 164-6
Asset registers 92-93, 167, 169, 191 en84
Audits:
    on employers 36, 95-6, 140-1, 144, 145, 147, 167
    on individuals 104, 144, 147, 148, 167
Basic Income 61-2, 68, 188 en53-4
Bequests, see Accessions
Bittker, Boris 97, 191 en81
Brennan, Geoffrey and Buchanan, James 122-3, 193 en94
Capital gains 8, 16, 87, 88

Changing the tax-rates:
   Automatically as a response to inflation 104-6
   By government 123-4
Children and lifetime taxation 20, 86, 100-4
CLIPH-rate tax:
   Explanation of 2, 77, 84-5
   Discussion of 117–120, 123, 125, 150-57, 159, 173–5, 182 en5, 195 en110
   Transition to 162–166, 170
Comprehensive income taxation: see CLIPH-rate tax, Tax base: Acquired income, Tax base: Comprehensive income
Constitutional rules and limitations 117-26, 129, 136, 165
Constructive realization 81, 91, 111-2, 192 en88
Consumption, see Consumption tax base, see Hourly averaging and prices
Corporation tax 96, 159
Counter-cyclical measures 71-3, 118-22
Crime reduction:
   through hour credits 41
   through the acquired income tax base 139
Death, see Constructive realization
Disability, see Additional hour credits: for disability
Dworkin, Ronald 4, 65, 181 en1, 181-2 en4-5, 187 en49, 188-9 en64-5
Earning subsidies 62-3, 188 en59, also see Hourly subsidy for low earners
Economic incentives and disincentives, see marginal tax rates and Participation tax rates
Economic rent 8, 29-30, 66, 69, 87, 185 en32
Employers
   Conferring hour credits 17, 36, 37, 137, 150, 184 en23-4
   Information required from and inconvenience to 53, 136-7, 139-41, 152, 166-7, 184 en22-4
   Of last resort: see Guaranteed work programme
   Of particular concern 85-6, 131-2, 143-9
Endowment taxation 6, 64-5, 188 en63

Fraud:
 Hour credit fraud 36, 44, 131-52
 Income fraud 94-7, 149-51
 Investigations 94-7, 126-8, 138-51, 166-7, 184 en23-4
 Punishments 46-7
 See also Audit
Gains: see Tax Base
Gifts:
 And the acquired income tax base 48, 55, 79, 85–87, 93–95, 166, 167,
 169, 189-90 en73
 Collusion 93, 138, 142, 184 en24
 Social fortune 5, 54, 55, 79,
 To children 101-3
 See also Partial gifts
Guaranteed work programme 38-41, 56, 68, 72, 127, 128
Hour credit:
 Nature of 2, 28, 37
 Calculations with 3, 9, 17-25, 26, 45, 53, 64, 66-8, 103, 105–107, 109,
 169, 177-178, 184en22 186 en39, 188 en 52,
 Fines 35, 46, 47,49, 137, 140
 Requirements on issuing employers 36-7, 138, 166-7, 184 en23
 Requirements on issuing managers 37, 127, 166-7
 See also: Additional hour credits, Fraud: Hour credit fraud,
 Maximum hour credits
Hourly averaging:
 And prices 29, 55, 68, 71-3
 See Hour credit: Calculations with
Hourly subsidy for low earners 14, 26-8, 55, 59
Income: see Tax Base
Inflation:
 Revaluating in response to 15, 87-8, 104-6, 121, 123-4
 Would CLIPH-rate tax cause? See Hourly averaging: And prices
Inheritance: See Accessions
Information on taxpayers:
 Information available to the public 95, 191 en80

Information available to agencies other than tax-authority 126
Information Technology and taxation: 3, 6-7, 19, 52, 91-93, 105
International Taxation:
Avoidance 154, 155
Competition 123, 154-6 157,
Global revenue sharing proposal 159-62, 194 en109
Helpful and intransigent states 163, 164
Investment returns 87–89, see Tax base: Acquired income
Kirchler, Erich 193 en96
Leisure 1, 8, 26, 28, 38, 43, 45, 68, 69, 83, 146, 183 en14
Leisure-lovers 22, 42, 54-6, 61-3, 68, 69
Lifetime Averaging:
Time based 14-7
Cumulative 15
True averaging 16, 17
Hourly based, see Hour credit: Calculations with
Marginal tax rate:
Effective Marginal tax rate 7, 29, 67, 182 en8, 185 en36,
Works differently with hourly averaging 33
Marriage: see Merging and demerging tax accounts
Maximum hour credits 42, 44-5, 136, 141, 145-6
Merging and demerging tax accounts 106-7, 113, 190 en74, 191 en87,
192 en88
Minimum wage:
Minimum wage with hourly averaging 27-9, 41, 72, 127
Minimum wage as a rival policy to negative hourly tax rates 63-4,
68, 188 en62
Minsky, Hyman 186 en42
Mirrlees, James 182 en8, 188 en63
Murphy, Liam and Nagel, Thomas 181 en1, 189 en64
Negative income tax – see Basic income
Negative hourly tax rate 26-8, 41, 68, 151
Nozick, Robert 181 en1
Online tax account: see Website for taxpayers
Overconsumption 72, 117–120, 128

Partial gifts 85, 87

Participation tax rate 7, 29, 67-8, 183 en13

Pensions 73, 108-10, 113, 193 en93, see also Retirement

Perquisites (Perks) 85

Phelps, Edmund 63,

Prices: see Hourly averaging and prices

Principles of a good tax system 4-8, 29, 51-3

Progressive taxation 5, 14, 15-6, 29, 57, 66, 68-9, 80, 96, 117, 156, 179, 182 en8, 185 en34

Public information, see Information on taxpayers

Punishment, see Hour credit: fines, see Fraud

Rawls, John 182 en5, 189 en64, 190 en76,

Real-time tax calculation 3, 111

Registers of assets, see Asset registers

Retirement 7, 68, 108-10, 182 en89, see also Pensions

Saez, Emmanuel 183 en13

Schanz-Haig-Simon tax base, see Tax base: Comprehensive income

Self-employed workers 17, 80, 145–148, 166, 184 en20

Simons, Henry Calvert 81, 190 en75, see also Tax Base: Comprehensive income

Smith, Adam 5-6, 182 en6

Smoothing of net income over time 14-15, 33, 58, 184 en20-1, 187 en51

Smoothness of tax-rate graph 30-2, 64, 67, 185 en33

Sovereign wealth fund 72, 117, 118, 120-2, 123-4, 163

Students see Additional hour credits: For students

Subsidies, see Earning subsidies, Negative taxation: Negative tax rate

Tax base:

Acquired Income 3, 20, 48, 84-97, 100-1, 111, 112, 118, 149-50, 159, 167, 169, 181 en2, 190 en78, 192-3 en92 see also Asset registers, CLIPH-rate tax

Broad-based 79-80

Comprehensive income (accretion, or Schanz-Haig-Simons) 81-2, 97, 101, 190 en7,

Consumption 2, 82-4, 91, 183 en15, 190 en76, 191 en79

Tax rates:

Constraints on these 30, 66, 177-9, 185 en34-6

Description and Graphs 18-9, 21, 23-5, 26-33, 66-8, 69, 107, 159-61, 177-9

See also Changing the tax-rates, Marginal tax rate, Participation tax rate

Tiebout, Charles 194 en106

Unconditional Income, see Basic income

Unemployment, see Guaranteed work programme

Vickrey, William 15, 57, 183 en16, 184 en19, 187 en50, 190 en77, 191 en87

Website for taxpayers 3

Wealth taxation 73, 77, 82

Wenzel, Michael 193 en96

Windfall taxation 5, 7-8, 16-7, 20-1, 24-5, 29, 69, 78-9, 82, 120, 183 en14, 185 en37, 189-90 en 73

Withholding of taxation 19, 53, 83, 92, 184-5 en26